ORTHODOXY
~ AND ~
HETERODOXY

Exploring Belief Systems Through
the Lens of the Ancient Christian Faith

ANDREW STEPHEN DAMICK

CONCILIAR PRESS ■ CHESTERTON, INDIANA

ORTHODOXY AND HETERODOXY

Exploring Belief Systems Through the Lens of the Ancient Christian Faith

Copyright © 2011 by Andrew Stephen Damick

All rights reserved. Printed in the United States of America

Published by Conciliar Media Ministries
PO Box 748, Chesterton, IN 46304

No part of this publication may be reproduced, stored in a retrieval system, or transmitted in any form by any means, electronic, mechanical, photocopy, recording, or otherwise, without the prior written permission of the publisher, except for brief quotations in critical reviews or articles.

Unless otherwise noted, all Scripture quotations are from the New King James Version of the Bible, © 1979,1980,1982,1984 by Thomas Nelson, Inc., Nashville, Tennessee, and are used by permission.

ISBN 10: 1-936270-13-7
ISBN 13: 978-1-936270-13-2

For Nicole

CONTENTS

"Now I plead with you, brethren,
by the name of our Lord Jesus Christ,
that you all speak the same thing,
and that there be no divisions among you,
but that you be perfectly joined together
in the same mind and in the same judgment."
(1 Corinthians 1:10)

Preface

This book did not start out as a book. It began its existence as a series of seven lectures first given for an adult education class at St. George Orthodox Cathedral in Charleston, West Virginia, in answer to a question from a parishioner at the cathedral: "What's the difference between Orthodoxy and other faiths?"

Those who are "professionals" (and I use the term quite loosely) in theological life may often be surprised to discover that what is so clearly and radically distinct to them may look fuzzy and undifferentiated to those who have not yet taken the time to peer more closely into the details of theology. I believe this surprise results from a modern situation in which theology is viewed as something only of interest to the so-called "professionals," not something that could present any interest to anyone else.

What I have found, however, is that most people actually are interested in theology, once the details are brought out, and particularly when it becomes clear that theology really does touch our everyday lives, that its shape shapes us in everything we do. This discovery became clearest to me when I first delivered the lectures that form the basis of this book.

Now that this work in its lecture form has been delivered in other venues, both at St. Paul Orthodox Church in Emmaus, Pennsylvania (my current parish), and via Ancient Faith Radio as the *Orthodoxy and Heterodoxy* podcast series, and most especially now that it's appearing in print, my intent for it remains the same: to answer for Orthodox Christians the question of what the differences between the Orthodox faith and other faiths really are.

I want to stress that this book's purpose is not to be used as a weapon against believers in other faiths, and shame on you who attempt it! This work

1

was written to educate Orthodox Christians, and while I imagine it may be read by people who are not Orthodox, they should realize that this book is not "aimed" at them, nor can its broad but nevertheless limited scope permit full justice to be done to other faiths' doctrines and traditions.

Although this book evaluates the content of other faiths' teachings, it is not an exacting work of apologetics. True apologetics is carried on by people much more qualified and learned than I, and I have no doubt that such people may read this book and easily point out various areas where it is not up to proper apologetical standards, whether they agree with my conclusions or not. For those interested, there are plenty of places to find such debates.

The foundational affirmation behind this work is that the Orthodox Christian faith is uniquely true, that it alone is the fullness of the revelation of God to man, and that the Orthodox Church is the same Church community founded by Jesus Christ through His Apostles. Because this much is assumed to be true, this book's treatment of other doctrines will never be satisfactory to those whose loyalties lie with those doctrines. (After all, if we agreed, either they would be Orthodox, or I would be whatever they are!) I have nevertheless tried to be as fair as I could.

My hope for this book is to introduce to Orthodox Christians the major elements of doctrine and practice that make non-Orthodox faiths different from Orthodoxy. More detail and nuance than this introduction provides can be found in other works, and I encourage those who wish to pursue those questions to continue exploring them. For those who want a "handbook" to what separates other major faiths from Orthodox Christianity, this (I hope) is the book for you.

Those familiar with the *Orthodoxy and Heterodoxy* podcast series should note that this book is not merely a print edition of the same work. While much of the material is the same, this book represents a revision, expansion, and (in some cases) correction of the material from the podcast.

Especially in that last regard, I am indebted particularly to two men who helped clarify a number of issues for me—Dr. Cyril Jenkins and Matthew Baker. Their ruthless reading of my manuscript was precisely what I needed. I am also grateful to all the people who showed up at the original lectures (in both Charleston and Emmaus) and challenged what I said, forcing me to think through some things more carefully and research them more thoroughly. Thanks also go to John Maddex of Conciliar Media, who (inexplicably) accepted the podcast for Ancient Faith Radio, and to the folks at Conciliar Press who have helped to refine this work in its written form.

I am most especially grateful to my wife, the Khourieh Nicole, who somehow always sees her husband's silly adventures as opportunities.

Introduction

Doctrine Matters

In most areas of life, we all are concerned with the truth. A cashier has to make sure he knows how much change he's giving. A nurse has to apply just the right amount of medication to a patient. A mathematician checks and rechecks his proofs. A jury listens closely to all the facts to sort out the truth in a trial. A history teacher has to get the names and dates right. A scientist publishes work for peer review to make sure that everyone gets the same results. In all of these cases and more, what's important is not opinion. Rather, it is truth.

Yet it seems that when it comes to questions of religion and spirituality and the accompanying moral questions, we as a culture quite suddenly become relativists. Instead of asking who God really is, we say, "Who is God to *you?*" Instead of asking what it means for God to have become a man, we suggest that that's okay for some people to believe if they want. Instead of asking whether God expects something from us, we judge religious expectations by what we ourselves want, by whether a religion fits in with us and our lifestyle. The pursuit of objectivity goes out the window, and subjectivity reigns.

This fundamental problem is compounded by the prevailing lack of familiarity with the tools of spiritual knowledge. That is, most people are not doing what it takes in order to see what is true. If an astronomer refused to use a telescope or a biologist refused to use a microscope, we would rightly regard such people as having, at best, incomplete knowledge in their fields. From the Christian point of view, what is lacking is purity of heart, as Jesus said: "Blessed are the pure in heart, for they shall see God" (Matt. 5:8). What is also lacking is proper guidance on how to attain that purity from those who have seen God and passed on this experience to the next generation.

5

Plato defined this same problem when he wrote *The Republic* and included the famous Allegory of the Cave. In this allegory, prisoners chained in a cave for their whole lives believe that the world is defined by the shadows they see on the wall. If one of the prisoners should escape and find his way to the surface, and then see the sun and all of reality for what it is, how would he be able to describe that experience to people whose whole experience is defined by shadows? And when he stumbles on his way back into the cave, trying to become reconditioned to life in darkness, those still chained to the wall may well ridicule him as having been damaged by his experience rather than enlightened. Such is the plight of many believers today.

Let me submit to you, therefore, that the great spiritual battle of our time is not a struggle between believers and atheists. Rather, it is a struggle between pride and humility. We expect and even demand humility in almost all other areas of life—what really matters is what is objectively true, not what any of us might happen to think is true. Our opinions are not what is important. Yet when it comes to ultimate questions about ourselves and the nature of existence, we set aside humility and place ourselves at the center of the universe. This temptation to pride is common even to believers in God.

One of the basic assumptions of this book is that Truth is not relative and that Orthodox Christianity represents the fullness of the Truth, the locus of the revelation of God in Christ. From that basic position we will be describing and analyzing various religious groups and their teachings, seeing what we share and where we differ. Because Truth is not relative, all human beings must be willing to set aside whatever we would prefer to be true and embrace only what really is true, changing ourselves, our attitudes, and our beliefs whenever necessary.

THE TRUTH BUSINESS

It has become unfashionable in our time to speak as though a particular doctrine is true and another one is false. Yet not too long ago, many religious groups in our culture regarded their own doctrines as true and also came to the quite logical conclusion that any doctrines which contradicted their own must therefore be false. Today, however, to come to this conclusion, and especially to speak publicly about it, is regarded by many as not being "loving," a word they usually use to mean "nice." Indeed, in our own time, a public disagreement over religion is sometimes considered "offensive."

And so, living as we do in an age of political correctness, we have been given new pieces of politically correct cultural theology which we are supposed to profess. This theology can be expressed with statements like these: "All religions are basically the same. What matters is that you live a good life." "We all worship the same 'God.'" "Religion is essentially a private matter. Don't try to 'impose' your beliefs on others." "I don't think any religion has it all right. We'll find out what's true when we get to heaven."

All of these statements are based on one common assumption: Beliefs about God and the ultimate nature of reality are not very important. That's why they should not be discussed publicly. That's why their details don't really matter. That's why we should not try to win people over to our faith. There really is no such thing as Truth. Everything is relative (except perhaps for the statement that "everything is relative").

And yet for nearly everything else in life, whether it's politics, health care, or even the Super Bowl record of your favorite football team, we demand seriousness, detail, and accuracy. Distracted with such transient things, we as a culture have successfully ignored a basic, yet obvious truth: *If there really is a God, then who He is and what He might want from us are more important than anything else in the universe.* It is on this basic assumption that this book rests. As believers, we are not in the "niceness" business. We are in the Truth business.

The purpose of this book is to examine the differences between the faith of the Orthodox Christian Church and the faiths of other Christian communions and of non-Christians. Obviously, as an Orthodox clergyman, I hold the position that the Orthodox Christian faith is uniquely true. I would not be Orthodox if I did not believe it to be the true faith revealed by God in His Son Jesus Christ. If I encounter a teaching of the Orthodox faith that makes no sense to me or strikes me as incorrect, then my conclusion should be that it is I who need to be reformed, not the Orthodox Church. This is in fact the classical view of all traditional religions, as opposed to the modern consumer-style understanding of faith popular in our culture: that each person is the arbiter of what is true and false, and that he is free to pick whatever bits of "spirituality" and belief he likes from a sort of religious buffet.

Just imagine, though, if we followed that approach in other areas of life.

What if we allowed doctors to pick whatever they wanted out of a smorgasbord of medical ideas and treatments? What if we ate whatever we wanted without regard to whether the food we choose is nutritious or even poisonous? What if we supported a politics based not on equality and justice but rather on personal feelings and opinions? If a relentless pursuit of truth is necessary in all of these fields, how much more so is it appropriate when it comes to questions of eternal significance?

The nature of Truth is that it is true no matter what anyone says about it. In the face of Truth, there is no opinion. Most people already believe that, but often don't apply it to the question that matters most, namely, "Who is God and what does He want from me?" But we all know that there is good, and there is evil. There is truth, and there is falsehood. This knowledge, based on our own experience in everyday life, should inform all of our thoughts and actions regarding what is ultimately true.

THE GOAL OF RELIGION

The purpose of this book is not to "prove" that Orthodox Christianity is the one, true faith. I do not believe that it is possible to prove any such thing, at least not by what can be written in a book. What we are seeking to do, however, proceeding from the position of the Orthodox Christian faith, is to show that the differences between Orthodoxy and other faiths are real and that they are important.

If you've ever visited the Internet website called Facebook, then you probably know that users of the site can put together profiles of themselves, detailing various bits of information about who they are and what they do. One of the details that can be specified is labeled as "Religious Views." Since I'm a user of the site, this feature has gotten me thinking on a number of occasions. This is what most people think of when they think about religion, that it's a question of "views." Religion is an opinion you have, something you think. Notice that Facebook doesn't even use the term *beliefs*.

But for most traditional religions, faith is not merely a set of "views." Rather, religious faith is a whole way of life, a purposeful way of living that has at its heart a certain set of goals that inform everything in that way of life.

In its terminology, Facebook is representing a secularist philosophy, which is not so much an outright denial of spiritual truths as a compartmentalization of elements of life into neat categories that have essentially nothing to do with each other. In this box, I keep my views on economics. In this one are my views on cable television. In this one, I have my reading preferences, and in this one, I keep my religion.

But even the word *religion* itself (which is not a word I usually prefer to use in reference to Orthodox Christianity) means something quite different. The word *religion* means "reconnection," to build and rebuild links. What you're trying to link yourself to will vary from one religion to another. But the key is that there is something happening here. It's not just something you think or agree with. And it's also not just about you. There is an "other" assumed by this process of reconnection. There's something out there, whether you call it God, gods, Brahman, the Force, a "higher power," or whatever. Religion therefore is not merely something you think; it's something you do, something that actively engages you.

Here is a fundamental truth about all religious practice: *What you believe and what you do make a difference.* If this is true, and I think it's obvious that it should be, then there is also a corollary we have to accept: *If you change what you believe and what you do, you will get different results.* This is true of everything in life. My big brother is a chemical engineer. My little sister is a biochemist. Believe me when I say that they know these things to be true. But if you don't know them, ask a doctor. Ask a physicist, a psychologist, a bricklayer, a janitor. They all will tell you that what you believe and what you do make a difference, and if you change those things, you'll get different results. What concerns me is that we so often don't apply this basic principle to what matters most in human life.

In a religious context, this fundamental truth means that different religions, because they believe differently and practice differently, will yield different results. Sometimes, those varying results are all put under one label, like *salvation*. But what does it mean to be "saved"? To a Hindu practicing religious yoga, salvation means release from the physical body and absorption into the oblivion of the universe, the annihilation of individual personhood in Nirvana. I guarantee you that isn't what salvation means to a Baptist. But what a Baptist means by that term and what an Orthodox Christian means by it aren't the same thing, either. Members of each of those faiths have different methods of trying to get where they want to go.

More than that, however, because there is truth and there is falsehood, and because most religions have traditionally claimed that their faith is true and that others are, by implication, at least somewhat false, then that means that some religious believers are fundamentally mistaken about their beliefs and practices. This means they're not going to get the results they think they will. We can't all be right, because we're making different claims about the nature of reality. In a room full of chemists all experimenting variously with the same chemicals, some will get useful products and others will get explosions in their faces.

THE NATURE OF TRUTH

In the Orthodox Christian faith, our purpose in life is to become more like Jesus Christ. The question of whether we "go to heaven" when we die is only one element in a much larger picture. That picture, ultimately, is of the Holy Trinity. An Orthodox Christian's whole life has one goal: union with the Holy Trinity, the Father, Son, and Holy Spirit, the one God who created all things. The path to that union is Jesus Christ, the God-man, the second Person of the Holy Trinity. Salvation is the attainment of eternal life.

In John 17, in Jesus' prayer to the Father before He went to His crucifixion, He defines what this means: "And this is eternal life, that they may know You, the only true God, and Jesus Christ whom You have sent" (17:3). He later prays, "And the glory which You gave Me I have given them, that they may be one just as We are one: I in them, and You in Me; that they may be made perfect in one, and that the world may know that You have sent Me, and have loved them as You have loved Me" (17:22–23). Therefore, in the Orthodox Christian faith, being saved—having eternal life—means knowing God in Jesus Christ. It also means receiving from Jesus the glory which, as the Son of God, He has from His Father.

From this, it's clear that salvation is about far, far more than whether we get out of hell when we die. It is a deep, intimate knowledge of God—Father, Son, and Holy Spirit. And in this deep knowledge—which is experience rather than the intellectual accumulation of facts—those who are being saved receive the very glory of God. Going to heaven or hell at the moment of death simply means that our experience of God in this life continues on to the next, but amplified. If we love God and know Him deeply, then our experience in the next life will be endless and intense joy. If we reject God or simply ignore Him in this life, then our experience of His love in the next life will be alien to us and felt as suffering.

This is why doctrine matters. This is why heresy is so very dangerous. It is because all of our doctrine is fundamentally oriented toward directing us to an intimate knowledge of God, because it is the character of our knowledge of Him which will determine our eternal path, our perpetual experience in the life to come. This knowledge will greatly depend on our adherence to correct doctrine and the living out of that doctrine in our daily lives.

Let me give an example I often use, which is a little coarse perhaps, but I've found it to be effective. Let us imagine that you are a member of my parish, and you heard a rumor that I was a practicing homosexual. Now, this is not true, but if you believe it, it will affect your relationship with me, and because I am a clergyman in your church, it may well affect the whole parish community.

Those who regard homosexual activity as a sin might become distant from me, and our relationship would break down. Those who are in favor of such activity might try to get closer to me, but that closeness would be on terms distorted by the false belief. Some might drift away from the parish entirely. Others currently outside might hear the rumor and never come for a visit, or instead might consider joining.

Those closest to me, my wife and my family, would be sure to have their lives very much disrupted if they believed the rumor. It would probably destroy our family life. And then the destruction of that family life would have reverberations not only in our extended family, but among our friends, the parish community, and so on. All because of a false belief about who I am.

Imagine the false belief were still serious but a little less extreme. Let's say that it was believed that I had a drinking problem. The effects of that rumor would probably still be significant, though nowhere near as explosive as the other. In any case, all those relationships are affected not merely by the moral actions of those involved—that is, whether they have done good or evil to each other—but by what they believe about each other and how they act on those beliefs.

Now, magnify all of those effects in proportion to the question of the worship and knowledge of the very God of the universe. Some false doctrines about Him can have major spiritual and even political ramifications. (If, for instance, you believed that the ancient Jewish temple in the modern state of Israel had to be rebuilt before Jesus returned to earth, wouldn't that affect not just your theology but also your politics?) Others are of lesser effect. But all of them, to one degree or another, take us away from a true, pure knowledge of the only true God, and that will affect whether and how we receive His glory and how we experience Him in the next life. Living a moral life according to the law of God is indeed critical for the life in Christ, but it is not enough. We must also know God as He has truly revealed Himself. That is why doctrine matters.

SOME TECHNICAL TERMS

All that being said, let me also say that we will all die ignorant, at some level, of who God is. No matter how much purity of heart and full truth in doctrine we attain in this life, God does not owe us life with Him in eternity. God will judge each of us based on what we do with the light we have received. All of us depend utterly on the mercy of God. Even the ability to be purified in this life comes from Him.

Because of this, we have to be clear on what various words mean that are used throughout this book. Within the Orthodox tradition, these words have specific, technical meanings (even if they are sometimes also used in non-technical ways), and we have to be careful how we use them. So here is a short list of terms you need to know when studying and discussing the question of Orthodoxy and heterodoxy.

Orthodoxy—Both "true teaching" (literally "straight doctrine") and "true worship" (literally "straight glory"). Orthodox Christianity is the life in faith given by Jesus Christ to the Apostles and then passed down within the Orthodox Church from generation to generation. It is not possible to be Orthodox outside the historical community of the Orthodox Church.

Heterodoxy—"Other teaching" and "other worship." Heterodoxy is anything that contradicts Orthodox Christian doctrine and worship. This term may also be used to refer to all non-Orthodox Christian groups.

Heresy—Literally, "choosing." Heresy is the act of choosing to be separate from Orthodoxy in doctrine and/or worship. The word may also be used to describe any heterodox teaching.

Heretic—One who was a follower of the Orthodox Christian faith and then consciously rejected it. Technically speaking, one who was never Orthodox cannot be a heretic. He may, however, believe in heretical teachings (i.e., heterodoxy).

Apostasy—Literally, "standing apart." Apostasy is the act of deliberately leaving the Orthodox Church. One who does so is an **apostate**.

Schism—Literally, "separation." Schism is a separation of a group from the Church, which may not include heresy on the part of the schismatics. (It often does, however.)

One

Orthodoxy, Heterodoxy, and Heresy

HOW THE ORTHODOX CHURCH VIEWS THE NON-ORTHODOX

It is part of the fundamental character of Orthodox theology that we do not theologize outside the Church. That is, although we have very detailed theology of what it means to be an Orthodox Christian, we have absolutely no theology about what it means not to be one. God has never told us the spiritual status of the non-Orthodox, except in only the most general terms which cannot be reliably applied to particular people. You can't find it in the Scripture, in the writings of the Fathers, or in the divine services. All we have been given is the Way.

From this, we can look at a given doctrine or practice and say, "That is not the Way." But we cannot say, "All of you who have embraced that heresy are therefore forever damned." We don't know that.

Orthodox Christians believe that the Way is Jesus Christ, the God-man, and that He founded a concrete, historical community, the Church, in which His followers live out the life He gave them through the work of the Apostles. Furthermore, we believe that the Orthodox Church is uniquely that one Church, that Christ did not found denominations or a movement called "Christianity." Historically, nearly all Christian groups have believed something similar about themselves and have also believed that other Christians were wrong in at least some aspects of their doctrine and practice.

It is clear from the point of view of Orthodoxy that not all religions are the same, that not all worship the same "God." (This observation ought to be obvious to anyone who takes religious believers at their word when they describe their beliefs.) Yet at the same time, we can recognize that there is truth in all religions and philosophies. St. Justin Martyr in the second century called this the *spermatikos logos*, that is, the Logos in seed form. The Logos, or "Word," is Jesus Christ (see John 1), and St. Justin believed that all belief systems had within them the seeds of His revelation. Because all human beings are created according to the image of God, that is, Jesus Christ, they are not capable of being wrong all the time.

This is why many who discuss the differences between Orthodoxy and other religions prefer to refer to those other faiths as "incomplete" rather than "false." Certainly, they usually have false elements, but it is a far better tactic to focus on what is true and show how that leads one to Orthodoxy, the fullness of God's revelation to mankind.

This recognition of the truth in other religions is what has led to the traditional Orthodox approach to the reception of converts. Some are baptized and chrismated (confirmed), some are only chrismated, while some are received only by profession of faith and confession, all based on the similarity to Orthodoxy of the baptism and faith of the group in question. This variety in practice is attested to even in the fourth century by St. Basil the Great, who goes on at some length in a letter to one Amphilochius about how different kinds of heterodox believers are to be received into the Church.

A saying from the twentieth-century Orthodox theologian Paul Evdokimov has become familiar to many Orthodox: "We know where the Church is; it is not for us to judge and say where the Church is not." This phrase is a helpful way of thinking about this question. From this saying, we can see that there are really two different questions when the Orthodox consider the non-Orthodox: the status of individual persons who hold to heterodox teachings, and the status of organizations that hold to heterodox teachings.

From the Orthodox point of view, all Christian and non-Christian bodies that are not Orthodox are fundamentally not the Church. The Church is a concrete, historical community founded by Jesus Christ through His Apostles, which has existed in a real community for roughly two millennia. That is why we can say where the Church is. In Emmaus, Pennsylvania, the Church is in one place—at 156 East Main Street. And of course the Church in Emmaus consists of all those people who belong to that community. That is, where the Church is in this earthly life can be answered empirically.

The question becomes more subtle when we're discussing individual persons. For any given person, whether formally a member of the Orthodox Church in this life or not, the critical question is whether that person will be a member in the next life. I am sure there are people who are formally Orthodox today who will not be so when they enter into eternity. I am also sure there are people who are today outside those formal boundaries who will be inside them in the next life. When it comes to individual persons, the only ones we know are Orthodox when it most counts—in eternity—are the saints. The saints are the people we know made it. We all live in hope, not in absolute rational certainty.

Describing Christian life as hope does not lead to a life of anxiety, wondering whether we can ever really "know" whether we're "in" or "out." It is much more like being married—it is always changing and evolving, but built on a certain foundation. There is always the possibility for greater depth and unity, but also for dissolution and separation. It is a dynamic relationship, not a static status. Just as we hope for ourselves, we also hope for the non-Orthodox that they would embrace life in the Orthodox Church in this life; but if they do not, we hope that when presented with God in the next life, Orthodoxy will be so clearly what they want that they will embrace it in that transition. We affirm that there is no salvation outside the Church, but ultimately whether one is in the Church is a question referred to the end of time. I have known more than one convert to the Orthodox faith who said of his heterodox parents after they died, "I believe they're Orthodox now."

So, while we can say with surety that heretical teachings are dangerous to the spiritual life, it is not up to us to judge any particular person in terms of how that danger affects him. We do not know, because none of us can look into another's heart. Nevertheless, because an Orthodox Christian believes that Orthodoxy represents the fullness of the Christian faith, he is called by God to share his faith with others, to invite them to experience that same fullness and be transformed by it.

It is absolutely essential, however, that all these discussions, while standing firm on what is true and right, be conducted with humility. The Orthodox evangelist must not say, "*I* am right, and *you* are wrong," because, after all, he refers to himself every time he takes Communion as the "chief of sinners" (cf. 1 Tim. 1:15). That the Orthodox Christian faith is uniquely true is not to the credit of any Orthodox person. We did not invent it, and we all fall short of living it as we should, because we are sinners. Thus, the Orthodox Church proclaims her heritage as the original Christian Church founded by Christ not in pride, but in humility as a historical experience.

ESSENTIALS OF ORTHODOX CHRISTIAN DOCTRINE

In order to be able to see heterodox doctrine clearly, we have to be clear on the essentials of Orthodox doctrine. What follows is a sort of expanded creed, a summary of what we believe as Orthodox Christians.

The Holy Trinity

- There is only one God, who created all things out of nothing.
- God is uncreated, existing before all created things, even time itself.
- God is three divine Persons (*hypostases*) who are one in essence (*homoousios*).
- The three Persons of the Trinity are all absolutely equal in deity, power, honor, and eternality.
- Each Person of the Trinity shares all that it means to be God with the other two, but none of what it means to be that Person with the other two. There is nothing that two share without the third also sharing it.
- The eternal source of the Godhead is the Father, from whom the Son is begotten and the Holy Spirit proceeds.
- God is essence and energies. God is absolutely transcendent and unknowable in His essence, but immanent and knowable in His energies. *Grace* is another term for God's energies.

Jesus Christ

- Jesus Christ is the Son of God, the Second Person of the Trinity.
- Jesus Christ is fully divine, by virtue of being the Son of God, begotten before all ages. He is of one essence, or consubstantial (*homoousios*), with the Father.

- Jesus Christ is fully human, by virtue of being the son of the Virgin Mary, begotten in time of her and incarnate of her and the Holy Spirit. He is of one essence/consubstantial (*homoousios*) with all of mankind.
- Jesus Christ is one Person (*hypostasis*) in two natures, the divine and the human. This union is the only *hypostatic* union in existence.
- Jesus Christ was born, grew up, taught and healed, was crucified and died on the cross, and then rose from the dead on the third day.
- Jesus is the Messiah prophesied in the Hebrew Scriptures.

Salvation and the Church
- There is only one Church, the Orthodox Church.
- The Church is the Body of Christ, a divine-human organism, of which Christ is the chief member and the only Head.
- Salvation is within and through the Church.
- Salvation consists of *theosis*, becoming divinized/deified, which means attaining union with God and becoming ever more like Him, becoming by grace what Christ is by nature. It is participation in the energies of God, becoming "partakers of the divine nature" (2 Pet. 1:4), but not participation in His essence. This process extends through all eternity, because God is infinite.
- Salvation rescues us not only from the guilt of sin, but from the very power of sin and death. It is not merely a change in legal status, but a change in actual being.
- Salvation is possible only by the power of God, with the cooperation of man—"by grace, through faith" (Eph. 2:8). This cooperation is termed *synergy*. God will always honor man's free will, so if man ceases his cooperation, then God's grace is rendered inoperative. Cooperation consists in repentance of sins, prayer, and participation in the sacraments.
- The Holy Mysteries (sacraments) truly communicate grace by the action of God Himself through the clergy, who are the servants of the mysteries, not their masters. The clergy are, through the episcopacy, in the succession of the Apostles, who were ordained by Christ.
- Christ will return again to earth, which will be the end of time and of reality as we now know it. All those who remain alive in the earthly life

will then be transitioned into the next life, where everyone else awaits them. All the dead will then rise again, reuniting their bodies with their souls eternally. Everyone will be judged according to what they did in this life.

MAJOR HISTORICAL HERESIES

Examining non-Orthodox religions is made easier not only by a knowledge of Orthodox doctrine but also by a knowledge of historical heresies that have been rejected by the Church as contradictory to the revelation of God. Following is a list of major heresies, grouped roughly in chronological order.

Docetism—The teaching that Jesus was indeed divine, but that He only "appeared" to be man. This heresy is mentioned (though not by name) in the New Testament and also in the writings of St. Ignatius of Antioch. One of the ramifications of this heresy is a denial of the involvement of physical matter in our salvation (called *dualism*, the opposition of the spiritual to the physical). The Docetists would therefore abstain from the Eucharist.

Judaizing—The teaching that Gentiles first had to become Jews before becoming Christians and/or that Christians ought to adopt more Jewish teachings and practices than the Church already had included. Judaizing is dealt with in the New Testament, being the occasion for the Apostolic Council in Acts 15. The Apostle Peter was initially a Judaizer (or at least sympathetic to that party), but was opposed by Paul (Gal. 2:11–21), whose teachings prevailed at the council. Judaizing continued in various forms for some centuries, particularly among certain groups known as "Jewish Christians."

Gnosticism—A broad term for a large group of different teachings. Almost all were dualistic (like Docetism) and included fanciful and complicated cosmological schema regarding the arrangement of the universe and everything in it. Most gnostic groups taught that a saving knowledge (*gnosis*) was what was necessary for salvation. They often also taught that only a select few were able to reach the highest spiritual plane and that most people could only function on a lower level. Those who ascended to this higher level had esoteric, "secret" teaching passed on from Jesus. Books like the *Gospel of Thomas* (a noncanonical work claiming to be from the apostle) are generally regarded as classic gnostic writings. The writings of St. Irenaeus of Lyons contain a detailed catalog and refutation of various gnostic teachings.

Marcionism—Marcion was a semi-gnostic heretic who taught that the creator God of the Old Testament was not the Father of Jesus Christ; rather, they were two separate "gods." To him, the Old Testament "god" was evil and capricious, while the New Testament God was loving and merciful. He was the first to put forward the idea of a Christian canon for the New Testament, rejecting the Old Testament. He included only books he regarded as fitting in with his ideas about God, including an edited version of Luke's Gospel (attributed to St. Paul and called the *Gospel of Christ*), as well as versions of some of St. Paul's letters and two texts attributed by his followers to Paul but not included in the Orthodox canon. He was excommunicated in 144 and established a parallel church hierarchy that persisted for some time.

Montanism—Followers of the "prophet" Montanus, who claimed to be the Paraclete (a traditional name in Orthodox Christianity for the Holy Spirit, usually translated as "comforter" or "advocate"). Claiming to receive revelations directly from God that fulfilled and superseded the revelation given to the Apostles, Montanus emphasized direct, ecstatic, and highly emotional spiritual experiences for all believers. Montanus was accompanied by two "prophetesses" named Prisca (or Priscilla) and Maximilla, who also claimed to receive visions from God, including the revelation of Christ in a female form. The Montanists did not claim to be messengers from God but rather claimed that God "possessed" them and spoke directly through them. The early Christian writer Tertullian fell into this heresy, being drawn by the severe moralism and rigidity of Montanist teaching. Montanism continued into the eighth century.

Manichaeism—Not strictly a heresy from Christianity, but rather a Persian gnostic religion begun by a "prophet" named Mani, which influenced a number of Christian groups and was the basis for several spin-off heresies.

Manichaeism was dualistic, as most gnostic faiths were, positing the existence of an evil creator god and a good, merciful god. The physical world is inherently evil and full of darkness, while the spiritual world is good and full of light. St. Augustine was a member of the Manichaean religion before he converted to the Church. Manichaeism persisted in various forms until the ninth century.

Sabellianism—Also known as **modalism** or **monarchianism**, this is the teaching that the Father, the Son, and the Holy Spirit are all simply "modes" of the one God. Sabellius (the founder of the movement) taught that Orthodox Trinitarianism was wrong in saying there were three Persons who were all God. Rather, he saw them as "masks" of one divine Person. Besides Sabellius, another major proponent of modalism was Paul of Samosata. Sabellianism is also called **patripassianism** ("Father-suffering"), because it posits that it was the Father who suffered on the Cross (since all three are really just one Person).

Novatianism—A rigorist teaching that believers who fell away during persecution or otherwise into serious sin could never be absolved. Novatian himself was an "antipope" (a non-canonical claimant to the episcopacy of Rome) whose teaching was condemned in 251.

Donatism—The teaching that the moral worthiness of a clergyman—most especially whether he had once betrayed the faith, even if he later repented—affects the validity of the mysteries (sacraments) performed by him. Condemned by the Council of Arles in 314.

Arianism—The major heresy of the fourth century and the occasion for the First Ecumenical Council in Nicea (325), Arianism taught that Christ was a created being rather than God. Founded by Arius (a priest of the Church of Alexandria), this heresy persisted for quite some time, even after it was condemned by the council in Nicea.

Chiliasm—The teaching that Christ will reign for a literal one thousand years on earth after His Second Coming. Chiliasm existed in various forms before the fourth century and was even taught in ignorance by some Orthodox writers, but it was finally condemned at Nicea with the phrase, "whose kingdom shall have no end," in the Creed.

Apollinarianism—The teaching (by one Apollinarius) that Jesus did not have a human soul. Rather, the divine Logos (Word) took the place of His soul. Condemned at the Second Ecumenical Council in Constantinople (381).

Pneumatomachianism—The teaching that the Holy Spirit is not divine, also called **Macedonianism** for its founder, Macedonius. The Pneumatomachians were so named because they "fought against the Spirit." Condemned at the Second Ecumenical Council with the expansion of the article on the Holy Spirit in the Creed.

Pelagianism—Attributed to Pelagius (though there is some disagreement as to whether he actually taught this), Pelagianism taught that man was capable of salvation without the assistance of divine grace. The major opponent of Pelagianism was St. Augustine of Hippo. Condemned at the Third Ecumenical Council in Ephesus (431).

Nestorianism—Taught by Nestorius, patriarch of Constantinople. Nestorianism teaches that instead of one Person with two natures, Jesus Christ was rather two persons "conjoined" together, one divine and one human. Nestorius thus refused to call the Virgin Mary *Theotokos* ("birth-giver to God"), but would only call her *Christotokos*, saying that she gave birth to Christ, but not to God. Condemned at the Third Ecumenical Council. The major opponent of Nestorianism was St. Cyril of Alexandria.

Monophysitism—Also called **Eutychianism** for its founder, Eutyches, Monophysitism taught that Jesus Christ was not "in two natures" but rather only "from two natures," forming a sort of hybrid nature which was half-God and half-man. (This teaching is distinct from the Miaphysitism taught today by the Oriental Orthodox churches [e.g., Coptic, Armenian, Ethiopian, etc.], which is regarded by many Orthodox writers as being consistent and compatible with Orthodox Christology. The Oriental churches also condemn Eutychian Monophysitism.) Monophysitism was condemned at the Fourth Ecumenical Council in Chalcedon (451).

Apokatastasis—The teaching that all will eventually be saved, even if they reject God. Condemned in 543 at a council in Constantinople.

Origenism—A complex set of teachings originating with the writer Origen (second century). Origen's main problems were cosmological and largely based on Greek pagan philosophical speculation (especially the works of Plato). Origen himself was never condemned in his lifetime, but his teachings later came to be such a problem that he was condemned by name in anathemas included in collections of the acts of the Fifth Ecumenical Council in Constantinople (553), which also condemned various Nestorian writings.

Monothelitism—The teaching that Christ had only one will, the divine will (rather than a human will as well). Taught by Patriarch Sergius of Constantinople and Pope Honorius of Rome, who were both explicitly condemned along with their teaching by the Sixth Ecumenical Council in Constantinople (680–681). The major opponent of Monothelitism was St. Maximus the Confessor.

Monoenergism—Closely related to both Monophysitism and Monothelitism, this heresy taught that Christ had only one energy, the divine energy, in opposition of Orthodox doctrine that Christ has both divine and human energies. Monoenergism was taught by most of the proponents of Monothelitism and also opposed by St. Maximus.

Iconoclasm—The teaching that icons are not permitted in churches. This teaching was condemned at the Seventh Ecumenical Council in Nicea (787) and primarily opposed by St. John of Damascus. It was not until 843 that icons were publicly returned to churches on the first Sunday in Lent (the Triumph of Orthodoxy).

Filioquism—The teaching that the Holy Spirit proceeds eternally not only from the Father (as stated in the Nicene Creed and John 15:26), but also "and the Son" (in Latin, *filioque*). The *Filioque* was first inserted into the Creed at a council in Toledo, Spain, in 589. It was again inserted into the Creed in 794 by the usurper-emperor Charlemagne (who also rejected the Seventh Ecumenical Council). The addition was finally rejected at a pan-Orthodox council (including legates from Rome) in 879–880 in Constantinople, a council regarded at the time, and by some Orthodox writers later, as the Eighth Ecumenical Council. The *Filioque* later was reinserted into the Creed by Rome and used as a charge of heresy against the Orthodox East in the Great Schism centered around the events of 1054.

Barlaamism—Taught by Barlaam of Calabria, who argued against St. Gregory Palamas. Barlaam taught that the hesychastic (from *hesychia*, "stillness") practices of Athonite monks did not actually allow them to see the Uncreated Light of God, but rather only a created light. He also argued that mental knowledge of God was the highest possible knowledge. He claimed that the philosophers had higher knowledge than the prophets. He was opposed by St. Gregory Palamas, whose theology was upheld at a series of synods held in Constantinople in 1341, 1347, and 1351, collectively referred to by some Orthodox writers as the Ninth Ecumenical Council.

Ethnophyletism—The teaching that the ethnic character of church members should determine the administrative governance of parishes and dioceses, i.e., that certain parishes were only for Greeks or only for Bulgarians, etc. Condemned by a council in Constantinople in 1872 after the question came to a head in Constantinople, where the local Bulgarian community had established its own bishop for Bulgarians.

Two

Roman Catholicism

DID THE GREAT SCHISM PRODUCE A NEW RELIGION?

A particularly close link already binds us. We have almost everything in common; and above all, we have in common the true longing for unity.

(Pope John Paul II, *Orientale Lumen*, 1995)

The Latins are not only schismatics but heretics as well. However, the Church was silent on this because their race is large and more powerful than ours . . . and we wished not to fall into triumphalism over the Latins as heretics but to be accepting of their return and to cultivate brotherliness. . . . We did not separate from them for any other reason other than the fact that they are heretics. This is precisely why we must not unite with them unless they dismiss the addition from the Creed filioque and confess the Creed as we do.

(St. Mark of Ephesus, 1439)

Like a branch that has been cut from a living tree, Rome had the outward appearance of life for many centuries after the Schism, even though lifegiving sap had really ceased to flow in her. Today, however, even the outward appearance testifies that this branch is indeed dead. . . . Pope John Paul II . . . must somehow shore up his Church, his papacy. He is now turning in the direction of the east and the ancient, historic Patriarchates of Orthodoxy. He is looking for a blood transfusion for his dying Church.

(Fr. Alexey Young, *The Rush to Embrace*)

Assuredly our problem is neither geographical nor one of personal alienation. Neither is it a problem of organizational structures, nor jurisdictional arrangements. Neither is it a problem of external submission, nor absorption of individuals and groups. It is something deeper and more substantive. The manner in which we exist has become ontologically different. Unless our ontological transfiguration and transformation toward one common model of life is achieved, not only in form but also in substance, unity and its accompanying realization become impossible. No one ignores the fact that the model for all of us is the person of the Theanthropos (God-Man) Jesus Christ. But which model? No one ignores the fact that the incorporation in Him is achieved within His body, the Church. But whose church?

> (Ecumenical Patriarch Bartholomew I, speech at Georgetown University, Oct. 21, 1997)

THE GREAT SCHISM

On July 16 in the year 1054, just as prayer was nearly begun in the great church of Hagia Sophia ("Holy Wisdom") in Constantinople, then the capital of the Roman Empire, three representatives of the Pope of Rome, led by Cardinal Humbert of Marmoutiers, entered the building. With Humbert were Archbishop Peter of Amalfi and Cardinal Deacon Frederick of Lotharingia (who in 1057 would become Pope Stephen IX). All three prelates were major leaders in papal reform, preparing for its later flowering under Pope Gregory VII (r. 1073–1089).

The three walked directly to the sanctuary containing the holy altar and threw upon it a papal bull excommunicating Michael Cerularius, the Patriarch of Constantinople. They exited immediately thereafter. Upon leaving the church, Humbert shook the dust off his feet and said, "Let God look and judge." One of the deacons of the church ran after the papal legates and enjoined them to change what they had done. The cardinal rejected his pleas, and the bull was dropped in the street.

Ironically, the pope himself had died on April 19 of that year, thus technically rendering his legates' authority null. Yet the deed had been done, and it is to these events in 1054 that historians generally point as at least a major marker in the Great Schism between the two groups of Christians who came to be identified as the Orthodox of the East and the Catholics of the West.

By no means were the acts of that July day in eleventh-century Constantinople the sole or defining moment in the Great Schism, but they have nonetheless become iconic in the most tragic and painful of all the breaks that have ever wracked Christendom. Numerous developments over several centuries led to that moment, and not until the early thirteenth century was the break recognizably complete. The centuries succeeding that day in 1054 have yielded two very different visions of what it means to be truly Christian, what it means to be the Church. These differences are not only in terms of mindset and vision, but also in core doctrines that are regarded as central to salvation itself.

DIFFERENCES IN VISION

There are three primary areas in which Roman Catholicism differs from Orthodoxy not specifically in doctrinal terms, but in terms of its overall vision, its theological and spiritual culture. These three areas are the development of doctrine, the relationship between faith and reason, and a different kind of spirituality.

Development of Doctrine

That the Roman Catholic Church accepts development of doctrine means that, as history progresses, new doctrines appear that were absent in previous centuries. Because the Roman Catholic faith is not "backwards compatible" (to borrow a software term), that means that a "good Catholic" from two hundred years ago could be in danger of excommunication were he alive today. For example, papal infallibility was denied by many Catholics, including bishops, until the official definition of the dogma in 1870 at the First Vatican Council. They all remained "good Catholics" before 1870. Now they would be excommunicated and under the anathema (curse) of the First Vatican Council.

Orthodoxy, however, believes in the development of the *expression* of Christian doctrine, but not of its meaning and substance, which is eternal, having been given by God in its wholeness to the Apostles. Further, although it is often the starting point for further theological reflection, Orthodox dogmatic formulation, especially in its conciliar expression, is primarily a pastoral response to heresy, not an opportunity for codifying speculation or systematic imagination in doctrine. Orthodox dogma never claims to expound the whole truth about anything, but only delineates the borders of the mystery.

The classic text on doctrinal development is John Henry Newman's *An Essay on the Development of Christian Doctrine*. Cardinal Newman, a nineteenth-century convert to Catholicism from the Anglican Church (and now on track for canonization by Rome), sought to defend his church against Anglican and Protestant attacks on Roman Catholic doctrines which were absent from the Scriptures and from the testimony of the ancient Church.

Newman himself would not have accepted the idea that truly new dogmas were being defined by the Church, and so his notion of the development of doctrine is similar to that of Orthodoxy, in which doctrinal expression develops, but its substance does not. Therefore, while Rome does not formally teach that doctrinal substance develops over time, the material evidence of Rome's doctrinal history (as with the immaculate conception or papal infallibility) demonstrates that it does indeed introduce new dogmas that were not held by the Apostles or the Fathers.

While it is true that some of the early Fathers held beliefs that were later rejected as incompatible with Orthodoxy (such as St. Irenaeus's chiliasm or St. Gregory of Nyssa's belief in apokatastasis), those personal opinions (no matter how boldly stated) were never the faith of the whole Church. With Rome, it is clear that the faith of the whole Roman Catholic Church has indeed changed.

We have to conclude that in Rome's model, Christ must have given only a "seed" of faith to the Apostles, which has grown and changed over time. Therefore, the Roman Catholic Church of today supposedly better understands the truth and has a higher level of knowledge than the Church of yesteryear. Thus, the post-apostolic Fathers had a higher level of understanding than the Apostles, the medieval Scholastics understood better than the Fathers, and so on. This theological background is the framework for all the innovations in Roman Catholic doctrine that differ from Orthodoxy.

Faith and Reason

Development of doctrine is possible in part because of the relationship Rome sees between faith and reason, in which reason is placed on a much higher level in Christian life than it is in Orthodoxy. Especially since the time of Thomas Aquinas (thirteenth century), Rome has defined and redefined much of its doctrine (often new dogmas) in terms of reason. Aquinas's project was to merge Catholic dogma with the philosophical requirements of Aristotelian logic. This merger is the origin of most modern Christian attempts to "prove" God's existence—which are based on the proposition that all doctrine must be logical and scientific in order to be believable. (Interestingly, Newman wrote in his *An Essay in Aid of Grammar of Assent* that strict paper logic was not enough for functioning in concrete life, including religious belief.)

Pope John Paul II in his 1998 encyclical *Fides et Ratio* puts faith and reason on the same level as means to the truth: "Faith and reason are like two wings on which the human spirit rises to the contemplation of truth; and God has placed in the human heart a desire to know the truth—in a word, to know himself—so that, by knowing and loving God, men and women may also come to the fullness of truth about themselves."

This kind of language is the reason Orthodox critics of Roman Catholicism describe it as *rationalist*—not just rational, but subjected to the demands of human rationality. Human reason becomes not merely a tool but rather the very criterion of truth. It is also the reason much of Roman Catholic spiritual life is *legalist*, because it is mainly concerned with satisfying legal, philosophical categories rather than addressing and healing spiritual realities.

For the Orthodox, rational thought is a useful tool to support the only true means of knowing the truth: faith in cooperation with God's grace. Reason, though useful, is not a necessary element in Christian life. Orthodoxy is rational, but not rationalist. You can be a true theologian in the Orthodox Church and yet be mentally retarded, because true theology is not defined by the acuity of the rational mind, but by the quality of the prayer of the heart.

Spirituality

The overemphasis on reason leads to an imbalanced spirituality (the everyday spiritual life of the Christian), in which the integral oneness of the body, mind, and soul that Orthodox spirituality nurtures becomes fragmented, and the body is too highly emphasized in spiritual life. Roman Catholic spirituality is therefore highly anthropocentric and materially focused. Instead of turning the eye of the soul away from this world, Roman Catholic spirituality tends to focus on specifically earthy images and sensations.

In the religious arts, some visual examples of this kind of emphasis include

Renaissance and Baroque art, with their highly sensual (and even erotic) character, and the realistic, three-dimensional statuary that is standard in church ornamentation. Orthodox iconography is deliberately non-realistic, to take the viewer away from this world and to the world beyond.

Roman Catholicism has also (at least before the modern introduction of Protestant-style pop and folk music) been home to a complicated musical style whose focus is not on the texts being delivered but on the ornateness of the harmonies and inventiveness of the composers, turning worship into a performance. Orthodoxy also suffers from this problem in some quarters (often through influence from churches under Rome), though both the East and the West have traditions of ascetical, modal chant. (The primary Orthodox chant of the ancient West is Gregorian.) Students of church music history will recall that harmony was in fact canonically forbidden in the early Church, precisely because of its emotionally manipulative appeal.

In private spiritual practice, we may think of the stigmata (bleeding on the body in the locations of Christ's wounds), the imaginative spiritual exercises of Ignatius of Loyola (the founder of the Jesuits), self-flagellation, and other extreme forms of asceticism. All of these represent a highly fleshy and sensualistic approach to spiritual life. They are focused on the flesh and on the imagination, sometimes almost in a magical sense.

Consider the popular Lenten devotion, the Stations of the Cross, which are dedicated precisely to imagining being present with Jesus at various points during His Passion. Also think of the popular devotional scapulars, little pieces of cloth that may be simply mnemonic tools to help the user remember to pray, but that may also be believed to have nearly magical powers—piously wearing the brown scapular is claimed to garner rescue by the Virgin Mary from purgatory on the first Saturday after the wearer's death (the "Sabbatine Privilege").

Roman Catholic spirituality is also characterized by the legalism required by its rationalist theology. For instance, it is held as a sin not to fast, whereas Orthodoxy recognizes fasting as simply a tool. One may also find detailed lists of how to obtain indulgences out of purgatory, quantitative penances ("Say ten Hail Marys and one Our Father"), and the annulment of marriages.

This problem really struck home for me when I was once looking at the big, old Catholic Bible of a college girlfriend. Inside the front cover was a detailed chart listing how many years out of purgatory you could get if you read so many minutes in the Bible. While this kind of thing is not emphasized as much in our own day, it is nevertheless clear that the daily Christian life of the Roman Catholic is not the same as it is for an Orthodox Christian.

THE PAPAL DOGMAS

What both informs and also is informed by these significant differences in theological and practical vision is a number of major differences in doctrine. Rome does not agree with Orthodoxy on such fundamental questions as ecclesiology (what the Church is) and the related role of the papacy. Likewise, our basic vision of who God is differs over issues such as the *Filioque*, absolute divine simplicity, and created grace. Even the question that most Christians eventually ask—"How are we saved?"—is answered differently by Rome's doctrines of whether non-Catholics can be saved; original sin; the complex system of merits, satisfaction, purgatory, and indulgences; and sacraments and "validity." We'll discuss all of these below.

The Universal Jurisdiction of the Papacy

Let's begin with the most widely known issue between Rome and Orthodoxy, the papacy, an issue which goes to the very heart of ecclesiology, what the Church itself is. Orthodoxy's objections to Rome's teachings about the papacy come in two parts, universal jurisdiction and papal infallibility.

Universal jurisdiction is the teaching that the Pope of Rome has supreme, immediate jurisdiction over every Christian, that he is the head of the Church. Any bishop or pastor may be overruled by the pope at any time, effectively rendering all bishops essentially vicars of the pope. Rejection of this teaching endangers both faith and salvation itself.

This teaching found its most explicit definition at the First Vatican Council in 1870:

> Wherefore we teach and declare that, by divine ordinance, the Roman
> church possesses a pre-eminence of ordinary power over every other church,
> and that this jurisdictional power of the Roman pontiff is both episcopal
> and immediate. Both clergy and faithful, of whatever rite and dignity, both
> singly and collectively, are bound to submit to this power by the duty of

hierarchical subordination and true obedience, and this not only in matters concerning faith and morals, but also in those which regard the discipline and government of the church throughout the world. . . . This is the teaching of the catholic truth, and no one can depart from it without endangering his faith and salvation. (*Pastor Aeternus*, Vatican I, 1870)

While it was Vatican I that gave such a clear declaration of universal jurisdiction, its teaching was not new to Roman Catholics. In 1439, when the Council of Florence met in an attempt to reunite the Orthodox Church with Rome by means of Orthodox submission, it declared, "The Roman pontiff is the true vicar of Christ, the head of the whole church and the father and teacher of all Christians; and to him was committed in blessed Peter, by our lord Jesus Christ, the full power of tending, ruling and governing the whole church." This kind of language goes even further back, and one can even find echoes of it before the Great Schism between East and West, though such overweening was most often rejected by the East.

The teaching that the pope has universal jurisdiction is also called *ultramontanism* because it gives the pope jurisdictional power "beyond the mountains" (i.e., the Alps at the northern border of Italy). (The term *ultramontane* has historically had other meanings in church usage, mainly geographic, e.g., referring to a pope who came from beyond Italy.) This dogma puts the pope above any council, above any other human being, and anathematizes (places under a curse reserved for heretics) any who reject this teaching:

The sentence of the apostolic see [i.e., Rome] (than which there is no higher authority) is not subject to revision by anyone, nor may anyone lawfully pass judgment thereupon. And so they stray from the genuine path of truth who maintain that it is lawful to appeal from the judgments of the Roman pontiffs to an ecumenical council as if this were an authority superior to the Roman pontiff.

So, then, if anyone says that the Roman pontiff has merely an office of supervision and guidance, and not the full and supreme power of jurisdiction over the whole church, and this not only in matters of faith and morals, but also in those which concern the discipline and government of the church dispersed throughout the whole world; or that he has only the principal part, but not the absolute fullness, of this supreme power; or that this power of his is not ordinary and immediate both over all and each of the churches and over all and each of the pastors and faithful: let him be anathema. (*Pastor Aeternus*, Vatican I, 1870)

If anyone hopes that the age of Rome making such claims might be over, he has only to look at the statements of its most recent officially ecumenical council, Vatican II: "In this Church of Christ the Roman pontiff, as the successor of Peter, to whom Christ entrusted the feeding of His sheep and lambs, enjoys supreme, full, immediate, and universal authority over the care of souls by divine institution" (Vatican II, *Christus Dominus*, 1965). This teaching is still very much on the books, and it is still in practice to this day.

This authority is taught to come from St. Peter, the chief of the Apostles, whose unique successor is the bishop of Rome. The universally supreme papacy is a necessary element for the constitution of the Church. Each local diocese is therefore only a portion of the Catholic Church and is not fully Catholic without submission to the pope.

This vision of Church governance is not merely administrative but involves a theological outlook different from Orthodoxy's collegial episcopacy. Students of American history will recognize a transition similar to the one in which centralized federal power won out in the Civil War against a looser federation of sovereign states. Just as Americans began thereafter to refer not to "*these* United States" but "*the* United States," Roman Catholics who refer to "the Church" most often have in mind the Vatican rather than a sense of the wholeness of the people of God. Supreme apostolic authority rests with one man.

Orthodoxy rejects papal universal jurisdiction on a number of grounds. First, we believe that Christ is the head of the Church, not any bishop (Eph. 1:22; 5:23; Col. 1:18). He also does not need a vicar (one of the pope's titles is *Vicar of Christ*), because He is always present in His Church.

As for St. Peter, there are some who see a special role for him when Christ gives him the "keys" to the Kingdom of heaven to "bind" and to "loose" (Matthew 16:19), but those same keys are given with a plural subject to all the Apostles in John 20:23. The Lord also describes Himself (not Peter) as having the "keys of hell and of death" in Revelation 1:18.

It is true that Peter was the chief of the Apostles, and the Orthodox Church honors him precisely in that manner, but the honor of sitting on the "chair of Peter" does not descend only to the Pope of Rome, but to all Orthodox bishops. Ironically, there is no historical evidence that Peter was ever the bishop of Rome, though he is celebrated as the first bishop of Antioch (Rome itself even has a feast on February 22 dedicated to Peter's episcopacy in Antioch!).

Peter is never called the head of the Church in any sense in the Bible, nor does he himself ever appeal to any supposed papal authority, even in his own epistles. Indeed, St. Paul did not recognize such an authority when he "withstood [Peter] to his face" over Peter's temporary acceptance of Judaizing (Gal. 2:11). At the moment when we would imagine Peter would be at his most papal, the Apostolic Council in Acts 15, it is James (the local bishop in Jerusalem, whose territory they were in) who pronounces the sentence of the council (Acts 15:13–21), not Peter.

The Church's history shows that councils trump the papacy again and again. None of the ecumenical councils prior to the Great Schism ever recognized the supposed universal jurisdiction of the pope. Even at the Fourth Council in Chalcedon (451), Pope Leo's *Tome* was not simply accepted but was rather reviewed and discussed first. The same council also defined Rome's primacy as primarily of honor (not of universal jurisdiction) and said in Canon 28 that the honor adhered to Rome "because it was the imperial city" (neither Peter nor any divine institution is mentioned). There are multiple ancient examples of various bishops standing up to Rome and not recognizing any supposed absolute and universal jurisdiction (e.g., St. Cyprian of Carthage against Pope Stephen over whether heretical baptism was efficacious).

Rome's claims to universal jurisdiction also present some practical and theological problems. Realistically speaking, if the pope has immediate and absolute authority everywhere, then he is essentially the only real bishop in the Church. All other bishops are effectively only vicars. St. Gregory the Great (Pope of Rome 590–604) recognized this as a theological problem when he spoke out against the new title Ecumenical Patriarch, which began to be used by the archbishop of Constantinople: "Whoever calls himself universal bishop, or desires this title, is, by his pride, the precursor to the Antichrist." He misunderstood what "ecumenical" was supposed to mean (it was a reference to Constantinople being the center of the *Ecumeni*, the Roman Empire), but he clearly rejected the idea of a bishop of bishops.

Another practical problem from this structure which has theological implications is that Catholicity is defined purely by submission to Rome, whose uni-
versality is the definition for true ecclesiology. But *katholikos* (the Greek word
from which *catholic* comes) does not properly mean "universal" but rather, literally, "according to the whole." For Orthodoxy, this wholeness resides in every
diocese with its bishop as the president at the Eucharist, surrounded by his
clergy and faithful. Orthodox parishes and dioceses are not merely part of the
Catholic Church, but rather manifest catholicity within themselves fully and
locally.

The claim to universal jurisdiction is even problematic within Roman
Catholicism, which has resorted and continues to resort (though in a limited
way) to conciliar solutions. A major example is the series of events known
in the West as the "Great Schism," beginning in 1378 and ending in 1417.
During this time, there were multiple competing claimants to the papacy—at
one point, three. This problem was solved not by an appeal to papal power
(after all, who was the real pope?) but rather by the Council of Constance
(1414–18).

This council not only solved the problem (by deposing two of the claimants, transferring one to another episcopal see, and then electing a new man
as pope), but it also officially taught a doctrine of conciliarism, declaring that
ecumenical councils were higher than popes: "Legitimately assembled in the
holy Spirit, constituting a general council and representing the Catholic church
militant, it has power immediately from Christ; and that everyone of whatever
state or dignity, even papal, is bound to obey it in those matters which pertain
to the faith, the eradication of the said schism and the general reform of the said
church of God in head and members."

Ironically, this council is regarded as the Fifteenth Ecumenical Council by
Rome, but it cannot be ecumenical by virtue of valid papal authority, since it
was called by Anti-pope John XXIII. Rome accepts the solution to the schism
that the council decided upon, but it rejects as "invalid" the session that put
forward the decree of conciliarism and distorts the constitution of the council
in order to preserve its doctrine of universal jurisdiction.

We also have to wonder: If a divinely instituted papacy is necessary for the
existence of the Church, what happens to the Church in the period between the
death of one pope and the election of the next, which Rome calls *sede vacante*

("the see is vacant")? Rome's canonists say that episcopal powers revert to the cathedral chapter on the death of the bishop, which therefore puts papal power in the hands of the College of Cardinals—an interestingly conciliar solution to such a problem.

Papal Infallibility

The second of the two papal dogmas (and the one probably best known) is *papal infallibility*. The pope is held to be infallible in questions of faith and morals when speaking *ex cathedra* ("from the throne"), a power held by the papacy since St. Peter. This dogma was solemnly defined by the First Vatican Council in 1870:

> This see of St. Peter always remains unblemished by any error, in accordance with the divine promise of our Lord and Saviour to the prince of his disciples....
>
> This gift of truth and never-failing faith was therefore divinely conferred on Peter and his successors in this see so that they might discharge their exalted office for the salvation of all....
>
> We teach and define as a divinely revealed dogma that when the Roman Pontiff speaks *ex cathedra*, that is, when, in the exercise of his office as shepherd and teacher of all Christians, in virtue of his supreme apostolic authority, he defines a doctrine concerning faith or morals to be held by the whole Church, he possesses, by the divine assistance promised to him in blessed Peter, that infallibility which the divine Redeemer willed his Church to enjoy in defining doctrine concerning faith or morals. Therefore, such definitions of the Roman Pontiff are of themselves, and not by the consent of the Church, irreformable. So then, should anyone, which God forbid, have the temerity to reject this definition of ours: let him be anathema. (Vatican I, 1870)

The pope is therefore held to have a personal gift from the Holy Spirit which protects him from teaching heresy, and his pronouncements are not subject to any review or consent by the Church. It does not mean that the pope is considered sinless or perfect in everything he says; this special gift is purely doctrinal in character.

Papal infallibility, however, suffers from historical problems, both in the

Scripture and in subsequent Christian history. First, as mentioned above, St. Peter's supposed infallibility was never appealed to during the Judaizing controversy; indeed, he himself was in the wrong until corrected by Paul. This infallibility is also mentioned nowhere in Scripture.

In the sixth century, Pope Honorius was anathematized as a Monothelite heretic by the Fifth Ecumenical Council. (Honorius officially supported Monothelitism in a letter he wrote to Patriarch Sergius of Constantinople.) This anathema was repeated by popes after the council, which makes one wonder who was infallible—Honorius or the popes who denounced him? Likewise, Pope John VIII in the ninth century condemned the addition of the *Filioque* to the Nicene Creed, but he was overruled by his successors in the eleventh century. Which popes were infallible? Other popes also famously waffled on heresy—Liberius, Zosimus, and Vigilius.

An infallible pope also makes councils to decide doctrinal questions entirely pointless, yet Christian history is filled with councils. Rather than go to all the expense of transporting hundreds of bishops and using up months and sometimes years of their time, why did they not just write to the pope to ask him to decide the question? These many councils (which fill even the history of Roman Catholicism) often speak boldly without any sense that they are merely advisors to the pope.

Even assuming papal infallibility is true, there is no single, agreed-upon list of infallible statements made by the pope, thus rendering this dogma almost useless in practice. There is no official formula which all Roman Catholics agree indicates an infallible, *ex cathedra* statement.

None of this is a problem for Orthodoxy, which places infallibility in the whole body of the Church, not in the hands of one man, no matter how exalted his position. At its base, papal infallibility stems from a need for epistemological certainty (absolute mental surety) and is another symptom of the legalism of Roman Catholic theology—the institution of the papacy is bolstered by a Western psychological desire for absolute assurance.

A Different God?

Orthodox Christians who look seriously at Roman Catholic dogma may even come to question whether we believe in the same God. Such a suggestion is not made lightly, but there are three Roman Catholic doctrines that set the Vatican's view of God apart from that of Orthodoxy: the *Filioque*, absolute divine simplicity, and created grace.

The Filioque

The *Filioque* (Latin, "and the Son") is an addition to the Nicene-Constantinopolitan Creed that defines the eternal procession (origin) of the Holy Spirit as being not only from the Father (as is the wording of the original Creed and the Lord in John 15:26), but also "and the Son."

The *procedit* ("proceeds") in the Latin translation of the Creed can be interpreted more broadly than the more narrowly technical original Greek *ekporevetai*, leading some theologians to try to redefine this doctrine to refer not to the Spirit's eternal origin but only to His temporal mission (i.e., His saving work in time for mankind). This definition is indeed consistent with Orthodoxy and taught by some of the Fathers of the Latin West (even using the word *filioque*), as well as by the Fathers of the Greek East, though not using *ekporevetai* but *proienai*. Such an interpretation is nevertheless inconsistent with Rome's official doctrinal statements, which make it clear that they refer to the Spirit's eternal origins:

> We profess faithfully and devotedly that the Holy Spirit proceeds eternally
> from the Father and the Son, not as from two principles, but as from
> one principle; not by two spirations, but by one single spiration. This the
> holy Roman Church, mother and mistress of all the faithful, has till now
> professed, preached and taught; this she firmly holds, preaches, professes
> and teaches; this is the unchangeable and true belief of the orthodox fathers
> and doctors, Latin and Greek alike. (Council of Lyons, 1274)

This kind of language is likewise used in the current *Catechism* of the Roman Catholic Church:

> The Holy Spirit is eternally from Father and Son; He has his nature and
> subsistence at once (*simul*) from the Father and the Son. He proceeds
> eternally from both as from one principle and through one spiration. . . .
> And, since the Father has through generation given to the only-begotten
> Son everything that belongs to the Father, except being Father, the Son

has also eternally from the Father, from whom he is eternally born, that the Holy Spirit proceeds from the Son. (*Catechism of the Catholic Church* (CCC), 246, quoting the Council of Florence, 1438)

Although there have been some modern attempts to dismiss it, the *Filioque* is still the biggest theological problem between the Orthodox and Rome, because it concerns the very heart of Christian theology, the Persons of the Holy Trinity. The most damning charge against it is that it changes the words of Christ Himself: "But when the Helper comes, whom I shall send to you from the Father, the Spirit of truth who proceeds from the Father, He will testify of Me" (John 15:26).

The *Filioque* violates the perfect balance of Orthodox Trinitarian theology: Instead of any particular attribute belonging only either to the divine Nature or the Person, the *Filioque* grants an attribute to two Persons but not the other. For instance, unbegottenness belongs only to the Father, begottenness belongs to the Son, while procession belongs to the Spirit. Likewise, all divine characteristics (e.g., immortality, perfection, omniscience, etc.) belong to all three Persons. But if being the eternal origin of the Spirit's spiration belongs to both the Father and the Son, that subordinates the Spirit in that He does not possess something that the other two Persons do.

The addition of the *Filioque* to the Creed, besides being heretical, was also uncanonical and a sin against the unity of the Church. The Creed was professed and ecumenically ratified at the Second Ecumenical Council (381). It's also telling that several popes did indeed anathematize any changes to the Creed, most especially John VIII, whose legates were sent to Constantinople in 879–880 specifically to reinstate the deposed Patriarch St. Photius the Great and to reject the *Filioque*. The council they participated in there leveled an anathema against any such changes. Earlier, as the *Filioque* first came to be used in Rome, Pope Leo III famously had the original version (without the addition) in both Greek and Latin inscribed on silver tablets at the tomb of St. Peter.

Certain practical implications can be inferred from the theology inherent in the *Filioque*. Because the Holy Spirit is subordinated by this theology, His ministries are "quenched" (cf. 1 Thess. 5:19) and replaced in certain practical ways in the prayer life of believers and the administration of church life. Orthodoxy teaches, for instance, that Church unity and infallibility are both the ministry of the Spirit, but Rome puts those in the hands of the papacy. Likewise, Orthodoxy's dynamic spiritual life is replaced by legalism (2 Cor. 3:6: "the letter [of the law] kills, but the Spirit gives life"), and balanced asceticism gives way to a fleshy, materialistic spirituality.

For a highly detailed refutation of the Filioquist heresy, see St. Photius the Great's *On the Mystagogy of the Holy Spirit*, which includes a close study of how the teaching is not only heretical but even absurd (e.g., if the spiration of the Holy Spirit belongs to the Godhead and not the Person of the Father, then the Holy Spirit must spirate even Himself!).

Absolute Divine Simplicity

Even aside from the distortion of the Persons of the Godhead that the *Filioque* engenders, Rome also distorts the nature of the whole Godhead with the teaching of absolute divine simplicity. Orthodoxy teaches that God is both unknowable essence and knowable energies, based on the experience of the saints. Roman Catholicism, while not explicitly rejecting the essence/energies distinction, emphasizes the doctrine of absolute divine simplicity, a requirement from philosophical categories, defining God as a "substance." This view is not merely another way of affirming that God is one; rather, it insists that His oneness is an undifferentiated singularity, with no facets, aspects, or distinctions.

Rome's language affirming absolute divine simplicity can be found in a number of official sources:

> We firmly believe and openly confess that there is only one true God, eternal and immense, omnipotent, unchangeable, incomprehensible, and ineffable, Father, Son, and Holy Ghost; three Persons indeed but one essence, substance, or nature *absolutely simple*; the Father (proceeding) from no one, but the Son from the Father only, and the Holy Ghost equally from both, always without beginning and end. (Fourth Lateran Council, 1215, emphasis added)

> The Holy, Catholic, Apostolic and Roman Church believes and acknowledges that there is one true and living God, Creator and Lord of Heaven and earth, almighty, eternal, immeasurable, incomprehensible, infinite in

will, understanding and every perfection. Since *He is one, singular, completely simple and unchangeable spiritual substance*, He must be declared to be in reality and in essence, distinct from the world, supremely happy in Himself and from Himself, and inexpressibly loftier than anything besides Himself which either exists or can be imagined. (Vatican I, 1870, emphasis added)

In this doctrine, the essence of God (who He is in Himself) is identical with the attributes of God (what can be said about Him). In Christianity, it was first put forward by St. Augustine, who gets it from the Neoplatonist Plotinus. But both St. Dionysius the Areopagite and St. John of Damascus say that the essence of the Father is beyond even the category of "being" itself and therefore it is beyond all logical affirmations, even one such as simplicity.

Absolute divine simplicity is also expounded in detail in the writings of Thomas Aquinas, the great synthesizer of Catholicism with Aristotelian philosophy. Orthodoxy agrees in a sense with divine simplicity, that God does not have "parts," but with the Orthodox emphasis on salvation as *theosis* and on God as Persons (rather than as a "substance"), it makes much more sense to teach in terms of His unknowable essence and knowable energies than to dwell on a philosophical category like simplicity.

Some Roman Catholics point to the explicit formulation of the essence/energies distinction in the fourteenth-century writings of St. Gregory Palamas as evidence that the Orthodox believe in development of doctrine as well. But careful students of the Fathers will see such language, using the same terms with the same meanings, in the writings of St. Basil the Great, who wrote nearly a millennium before Gregory. This distinction is also in Scripture, though in other terms. Knowledge of God is knowledge of His energies, not His essence, which makes sense when reading passages such as, "No one has seen God at any time" (John 1:18; 1 John 4:12), in light of St. Peter's insistence that we can become "partakers of the divine nature" (2 Pet. 1:4), who through purity of heart may "see God" (Matt. 5:8).

Absolute divine simplicity is also the basis for the Roman Catholic doctrine of the beatific vision, in which man can only "behold" God in heaven but not truly become one with Him in *theosis* (divinization/deification). There is always a certain distance between the Christian and God. It should be noted, however, that *theosis* is not completely absent from Roman Catholic theology. Aquinas includes it in his writings. But *theosis* does not define salvation for Rome the way it does for Orthodoxy.

What is underneath this doctrine is Rome's greater interest in defining God's nature than in experiencing God's three Persons. Our concrete experience of God is as Persons, however, not of an independently existing nature. Absolute divine simplicity does damage to the theology of the person, sometimes even conflating person with nature.

We should be cautious here, though, because the question is mainly one of emphasis rather than absolute contradiction. (In theology, emphasis nevertheless matters.) If included as part of a full Orthodox Triadology, divine simplicity can be understood in an Orthodox manner, but Orthodoxy focuses more on God as three Persons—Father, Son, and Holy Spirit—than as a "substance," however defined. The question for the Orthodox is not really, "What is God?" but rather, "Who is God?"

Created Grace

If God is supposedly absolutely simple and absolutely transcendent, then union with Him is impossible. This leads to the doctrine of created grace, because there needs to be some sort of created intermediary between God and man.

Roman Catholic theology teaches that there is both uncreated grace (i.e., God) and created grace (although this precise term is not usually used). Created grace may be plural (i.e., "graces") and designates created effects from God. It is this created grace that resides in the human person and becomes a quality of his nature. It is "granted" or "conferred." This grace can give "merit" or a "disposition" to the believer. Uncreated grace may therefore be thought of as a cause, while created grace is an effect.

In the classic sense from the Scholastics, created grace is used in an "analogical" sense rather than an absolute one, meaning that these "merits" given to man are understood as "grace" only by analogy to God's work. While this formulation should rightly make Orthodox uncomfortable (how can grace have an analogue?), "created grace" language is used in some of the Orthodox Fathers. In practice, however, this more balanced theological formulation is largely swallowed up in the Latin insistence on "merit," especially from the Council of Trent (1545–63) until the twentieth century.

Nevertheless, "created grace" language still finds its place in the current *Catechism*:

> Sanctifying grace is an habitual gift, a stable and supernatural disposition
> that perfects the soul itself to enable it to live with God, to act by his
> love. *Habitual grace*, the permanent disposition to live and act in keeping
> with God's call, is distinguished from actual graces which refer to God's
> interventions, whether at the beginning of conversion or in the course of the
> work of sanctification. (CCC, 2000)

> Sanctifying grace is the gratuitous gift of his life that God makes to us; it is
> infused by the Holy Spirit into the soul to heal it of sin and to sanctify it.
>   Sanctifying grace makes us "pleasing to God." Charisms, special graces
> of the Holy Spirit, are oriented to sanctifying grace and are intended for the
> common good of the Church. God also acts through many actual graces,
> to be distinguished from habitual grace which is permanent in us. (CCC,
> 2023–24)

This approach contrasts with the main emphasis in Orthodox doctrine, in which divine grace is all uncreated and therefore represents the actual presence of God Himself in the believer. That which sanctifies the believer, by synergy (God and man working together), is the energies of God. There is nothing in the believer's person that sanctifies himself.

Likewise, if the grace the believer experiences is simply an "effect," "quality," or "disposition," then he remains separate from God. The indwelling of the Holy Spirit will always have a certain distance to it. There is no true union.

It should be noted that not all Roman Catholics accept the doctrine of created grace. The Franciscans never accepted it, and many Jesuits assert that Thomas Aquinas also did not teach it. In the modern era, Henri Cardinal de Lubac (one of the *Ressourcement* theologians) says that created grace and the accompanying strong emphasis on the division between grace and nature actually lead to secularism.

Salvation of Non-Catholics
If differences in belief concerning the nature of the Church and the identity of God were not enough to separate Roman Catholicism from Orthodoxy, the

theology of salvation itself is also markedly different. While Rome taught for centuries that submission to the papacy was required for salvation, it has softened this stance in recent years. That said, Rome's essential understanding of what sin is, how it affects mankind, and how he is saved from it is still radically at variance with Orthodoxy.

One question we are likely to ask is whether non-Catholics can be saved. The answer is unfortunately confusing, because Rome has changed its position on this question over the years. In the fourteenth century, we see this very strong language: "Furthermore, we declare, we proclaim, we define that it is absolutely necessary for salvation that every human creature be subject to the Roman Pontiff" (Papal bull *Unam Sanctam*, 1302, Pope Boniface VIII). Clearly, anyone not submitting to Rome is damned. This same language is used in the sixteenth century: "It is of the necessity of salvation for all Christ's faithful to be subject to the Roman pontiff" (Fifth Lateran Council, 1516).

Yet while criticizing the Orthodox in fairly strong terms, early twentieth-century Catholic theologians saw Rome's relationship with the East as an actual division within Christendom, not only as the East having left Rome:

> It is not Latins, it is they [i.e., the Orthodox] who have left the Faith of their Fathers. There is no humiliation in retracing one's steps when one has wandered down a mistaken road because of long-forgotten personal quarrels. They too must see how disastrous to the common cause is the scandal of the division. They too must wish to put an end to so crying an evil. And if they really wish it the way need not be difficult. For, indeed, after nine centuries of schism we may realize on both sides that it is not only the greatest it is also the most superfluous evil in Christendom. (*Catholic Encyclopedia*, "Eastern schism," 1913)

By the time we get to the Second Vatican Council, Rome is explicitly teaching that non-Catholics have the possibility to be saved:

> Those who, through no fault of their own, do not know the Gospel of Christ or his Church, but who nevertheless seek God with a sincere heart, and, moved by grace, try in their actions to do his will as they know it

through the dictates of their conscience—those too may achieve eternal salvation. (Vatican II, *Lumen Gentium*, 1965)

Therefore, while Orthodox Christians in the fourteenth century would be assured by Rome that they were damned, they can now be covered by the "ignorance clause" of the language of the Second Vatican Council. Even apart from the question of which of these papal statements should be deemed infallible, such a shift leads one to wonder how Rome will change its stance in the future.

Original Sin

Following the teaching of St. Augustine of Hippo (whom the Orthodox Church venerates as a saint without endorsing all his doctrines), Roman Catholicism teaches that original sin is transmitted to the descendants of Adam and Eve by means of sexual reproduction:

> Whenever it comes to the actual process of generation, the very embrace which is lawful and honourable cannot be effected without the ardour of lust.... [This lust] is the daughter of sin, as it were; and whenever it yields assent to the commission of shameful deeds, it becomes also the mother of many sins.... Now from this concupiscence whatever comes into being by natural birth is bound by original sin. (St. Augustine of Hippo, *De bono coniugali*)

In another place, in speaking of the "duty" of sexual intercourse, Augustine says that married couples should only "descend to it with regret" (*Sermon on the Agreement of the Evangelists Matthew and Luke in the Generations of the Lord*, 25). The Council of Trent also made it clear that original sin is transmitted by sexual reproduction:

> If anyone asserts that this sin of Adam, which in its origin is one, and *by propagation*, not by imitation, *transfused into all*, which is in each one as something that is his own, is taken away either by the forces of human nature or by a remedy other than the merit of the one mediator, our Lord Jesus Christ, who has reconciled us to God in his own blood, made unto us

justice, sanctification and redemption; or if he denies that that merit of Jesus Christ is applied both to adults and to infants by the sacrament of baptism rightly administered in the form of the Church, let him be anathema; for there is no other name under heaven given to men, whereby we must be saved. (Council of Trent, *Decree on Original Sin*, 1546, emphasis added)

If anyone denies that by the grace of our Lord Jesus Christ which is conferred in baptism, the *guilt of original sin* is remitted, or says that the whole of that which belongs to the essence of sin is not taken away, but says that it is only canceled or not imputed, let him be anathema. (*ibid.*, emphasis added)

This same language is also used by the current *Catechism*:

How did the sin of Adam become the sin of all his descendants? The whole human race is in Adam "as one body of one man." By this "unity of the human race" all men are implicated in Adam's sin, as all are implicated in Christ's justice. Still, the transmission of original sin is a mystery that we cannot fully understand. But we do know by Revelation that Adam had received original holiness and justice not for himself alone, but for all human nature. By yielding to the tempter, Adam and Eve committed a *personal sin*, but this sin affected the *human nature* that they would then transmit *in a fallen state*. It is a sin which will be *transmitted by propagation* to all mankind, that is, by the transmission of a human nature deprived of original holiness and justice. And that is why original sin is called "sin" only in an analogical sense: it is a sin "contracted" and not "committed"—a state and not an act. (CCC, 404, emphasis added)

Much of Roman Catholicism's understanding of original sin stems from a mistranslation of Romans 5:12: "Therefore, just as through one man sin entered the world, and death through sin, and thus death spread to all men, because all sinned." In Latin translations, the last phrase is *in quo omnes peccaverunt*, meaning "in whom all have sinned," saying that in Adam (the "one man") all sinned, making all guilty of Adam's sin. In Greek, it is *eph' o pantes himarton*, "because all sinned," which is not only the actual wording of the Scripture but the faith of the Orthodox Church. That is, while we all suffer the effects of Adam's sin (because we are human), we are not guilty of any sins but our own. We did not sin in Adam, but we sin because Adam's sin made us capable of sin. That is why many Orthodox writers prefer to use the term *ancestral sin* rather than *original sin*.

Augustine's teaching that sexual reproduction is inherently tainted (despite being necessary for the continuance of the human race) goes against the clear sense of Hebrews 13:4, which says that the marriage bed is "undefiled." It is true that some of the Fathers say that the current physical modality of sexual reproduction is a result of the Fall (just like the natural world's chaotic state, e.g., earthquakes, hurricanes), but they do not say that sex is itself sinful.

The Immaculate Conception

The original sin doctrine is also the origin of the *immaculate conception* teaching, which says that the Virgin Mary was preserved from all stain of original sin when she was conceived (declared as dogma in 1854, though rejected by Thomas Aquinas in the thirteenth century). Christ would therefore be born without it. Yet for the Orthodox, it is not guilt that Christ is born with, but rather mortality. He, like His mother, suffered the effects of fallen human nature (such as hunger, fatigue, etc.), but did not commit any personal sins. The original sin/immaculate conception combination puts Him outside of human nature, making Him not truly human. It also makes Mary's personal holiness no great achievement, since she would be rendered incapable of sin from conception. The clearest argument against the immaculate conception, however, is that the Virgin Mary died. If she had been born without original sin, then she would have been incapable of death.

Because of its understanding of original sin in legal terms, sin and death are primarily conceived of in Roman Catholic doctrine as a debt or as a crime against God. Further, even if the believer is forgiven his sins, he still has to pay for them with temporal punishment. God supposedly requires satisfaction both for the guilt of the sin and for the debt that the believer owes God in payment, and the believer has to merit his salvation. He also has to pay the temporal punishment due for his sins in purgatory, the suffering of which may be lessened by gaining indulgences. The *Catholic Encyclopedia* puts it this way:

Sin, as an offence against God, demands satisfaction in the first sense; the temporal punishment due to sin calls for satisfaction in the second sense.

Christian faith teaches us that the Incarnate Son of God by His death on the cross has in our stead fully satisfied God's anger at our sins, and thereby effected a reconciliation between the world and its Creator. . . . It is a defined article of the Catholic Faith that man before, in, and after justification derives his whole capability of meriting and satisfying, as well as his actual merits and satisfactions, solely from the infinite treasure of merits which Christ gained for us on the Cross.

The second kind of satisfaction, that namely by which temporal punishment is removed, consists in this, that the penitent after his justification gradually cancels the temporal punishments due to his sins, either *ex opere operato*, by conscientiously performing the penance imposed on him by his confessor, or *ex opere operantis*, by self-imposed penances (such as prayer, fasting, almsgiving, etc.) and by bearing patiently the sufferings and trials sent by God; if he neglects this, he will have to give full satisfaction (*satispassio*) in the pains of purgatory. ("Merit," 1913)

Therefore, salvation is primarily a matter of "satisfying" God and averting His wrath against us. There is little emphasis on the healing and transformation of the human person. The idea that the Son of God became man in order to satisfy the Father's wrath finds its fullest expression in Anselm of Canterbury's *Cur Deus homo* ("Why God became man").

Orthodoxy, following the Scriptures, also uses the language of "debt" or "crime" in describing our sins against God, but it is not emphasized as it has been for Rome, nor is there any complex system of satisfaction, merit, and indulgences. The Fathers of the Church do not teach this idea of temporal punishment for sins, because forgiveness cancels out any kind of punishment. If God forgives someone, why would He still demand payment through satisfaction? This model denies the power of forgiveness in Christ's death and resurrection.

If God needs to be "satisfied," then He is capricious for having permitted us to fall into sin: He made up the rules knowing full well that we would break them. He is all the more monstrous in then demanding that His own Son be sacrificed in order that He may be appeased.

Further, in focusing on the legal metaphor language of salvation used in the Scriptures, Roman Catholics ignore the more dominant understanding of salvation in the Scriptures, which is healing. Even the very word *sozein* in the Greek Scriptures, which is translated "to save," also literally means "to heal." Salvation is healing, even in its basic definitional sense. With Rome's legalistic emphasis, however, personal change is de-emphasized. The main goal is therefore to attain a certain status, that is, a "state of grace."

Merit is also a concept totally foreign to the Orthodox faith. No one can "merit" salvation, not even the saints. It is not Christ's "merit" that saves us, but rather our participation in Him.

Purgatory and Indulgences

In working out what temporal punishment must mean, Rome has put forward the doctrine of purgatory. Purgatory is imagined as a place of temporal punishment where a saved believer pays God what he owes by suffering in torment for a certain number of years (while nonetheless somehow experiencing a joy not known on earth). Indulgences are obtained in terms of a certain amount of time out of purgatory.

In previous centuries, one could buy indulgences directly. (This was one of the main complaints in the Protestant Reformation. It was mainly through the sale of indulgences that the building of the Basilica of St. Peter at the Vatican was funded.) In many cases, masses are "bought" with a certain donation in order to help some friend or loved one out of purgatory.

Despite not being as well-known in our own day, the system of indulgences very much remains in place and is spoken of in detail in the current *Catechism*:

> An indulgence is a remission before God of the temporal punishment due to sins whose guilt has already been forgiven, which the faithful Christian who is duly disposed gains under certain prescribed conditions through the action of the Church which, as the minister of redemption, dispenses and applies with authority the treasury of the satisfactions of Christ and the saints.
>
> An indulgence is partial or plenary according as it removes either part or all of the temporal punishment due to sin. The faithful can gain indulgences for themselves or apply them to the dead.
>
> To understand this doctrine and practice of the Church, it is necessary

to understand that sin has a double consequence. Grave sin deprives us of communion with God and therefore makes us incapable of eternal life, the privation of which is called the "eternal punishment" of sin. On the other hand every sin, even venial, entails an unhealthy attachment to creatures, which must be purified either here on earth, or after death in the state called Purgatory. This purification frees one from what is called the "temporal punishment" of sin. These two punishments must not be conceived of as a kind of vengeance inflicted by God from without, but as following from the very nature of sin. A conversion which proceeds from a fervent charity can attain the complete purification of the sinner in such a way that no punishment would remain. (CCC, 1471–1472)

Indulgences are also still understood as coming from merits:

An indulgence is obtained through the Church who, by virtue of the power of binding and loosing granted her by Christ Jesus, intervenes in favor of individual Christians and opens for them the treasury of the merits of Christ and the saints to obtain from the Father of mercies the remission of the temporal punishments due for their sins. Thus the Church does not want simply to come to the aid of these Christians, but also to spur them to works of devotion, penance, and charity. (CCC, 1478)

One can also gain indulgences for other people: "Through indulgences the faithful can obtain the remission of temporal punishment resulting from sin for themselves and also for the souls in Purgatory" (CCC, 1498). It is because the temporal punishment for sins is understood in the legal category of "debt" that one can pay for such punishment for someone else:

The possibility of this transfer rests on the fact that the residual punishments for sin are in the nature of a debt, which may be legitimately paid to the creditor and thereby cancelled not only by the debtor himself but also by a friend of the debtor. This consideration is important for the proper understanding of the usefulness of suffrages for the souls in purgatory. (*Catholic Encyclopedia*, "Merit," 1913)

Even Pope John Paul II, who was not known for stressing traditionalism in the Roman Catholic Church, issued a detailed document on how to gain indulgences in the year 2000:

> The plenary indulgence of the Jubilee [i.e., the year 2000] can also be gained through actions which express in a practical and generous way the penitential spirit which is, as it were, the heart of the Jubilee. This would include abstaining for at least one whole day from unnecessary consumption (e.g., from smoking or alcohol, or fasting or practising abstinence according to the general rules of the Church and the norms laid down by the Bishops' Conferences) and donating a proportionate sum of money to the poor; supporting by a significant contribution works of a religious or social nature (especially for the benefit of abandoned children, young people in trouble, the elderly in need, foreigners in various countries seeking better living conditions); devoting a suitable portion of personal free time to activities benefitting the community, or other similar forms of personal sacrifice. (Papal bull *Incarnationis Mysterium*, 1998)

Orthodoxy agrees that there is a certain purgation needed for souls destined for heaven, but that experience has never been codified with the temporal model of years of suffering employed by Rome. To be absent from the body is to be present with the Lord (2 Cor. 5:8). The soul's cleansing as it enters heaven is also not understood as making any sort of payment to God, nor as a punishment for sins.

The biggest problem with purgatory is that it assumes a division of salvation into two parts: getting to heaven and being "purged" or paying off the debt of sin. The emphasis in spiritual life is then placed on externalized works in order to earn time out of purgatory rather than personal transformation in order to unite with God. Christ's saving work only suffices to get believers to heaven, but they still have to work themselves to be really free from sin.

In some sense, full forgiveness can only ever be bought, either with money or with good deeds. For Orthodoxy, it is even more nonsensical to suggest that one may essentially "buy" another person's spiritual advancement (by gaining indulgences on their behalf). We may affect another person's life by our prayers, but we cannot exercise any sort of critical control over their spiritual experience.

Purgatory also presumes a linear temporal model for the afterlife, but we have no indication from the Scriptures or the Fathers that there is "time" as we know it in the hereafter.

Validity of Sacraments

Rome's legalism also leads it to understand the sacraments in terms of the categories of created grace (see above) and of validity. If certain requirements are met, then a sacrament is "valid." Sacraments are thus objectified and may be removed from their traditional context, such as confirmation from the context of baptism, ordination from the context of service in the Church, and the Eucharist from the context of communion.

Probably the most significant difference in Roman Catholic sacramental practice which separates it from Orthodoxy is the delay of two vital holy mysteries: Holy Communion and confirmation (chrismation). Holy Communion is not given to all baptized members, but only to those above a certain age (usually seven). Confirmation is also usually delayed until sometime in the teenage years. These delays have their roots in the rationalism of Roman Catholic doctrine—the idea that a believer needs some form of rational understanding in order to receive these sacraments.

Delaying communion is especially rejected by the Orthodox. If a child is baptized and a member of the Church, why should he be denied the sacrament that unites us all together as one body? He is somehow not really a member, being baptized yet excommunicated. The delay in confirmation originally arose from the practice of the sacrament being administered only by the bishop. Since he seldom visited local parishes, and since a steady stream of baptisms was needed when babies were born, confirmation was separated out from the baptismal rite. But later, confirmation became delayed as a matter of principle, and now it waits typically until the teenage years, supposedly uniting those who receive it "more closely to the Church":

> In the Latin Rite, the ordinary minister of Confirmation is the bishop. If the
> need arises, the bishop may grant the faculty of administering Confirmation
> to priests, although it is fitting that he confer it himself, mindful that the
> celebration of Confirmation has been temporally separated from Baptism

for this reason. Bishops are the successors of the apostles. They have
received the fullness of the sacrament of Holy Orders. The administration
of this sacrament by them demonstrates clearly that its effect is to unite
those who receive it more closely to the Church, to her apostolic origins, and
to her mission of bearing witness to Christ. (CCC, 1313)

But what can it mean to be united "more closely to the Church"? For the
Orthodox, one is either a member or not. It has been said of Rome's practice in
delaying confirmation that it is a "sacrament in search of a theology." Since it is
delayed as a matter of course, it is not clear what it is actually supposed to do.
Orthodoxy (and Eastern Catholicism) maintains the tradition of chrismation
(confirmation) being part of baptism.

Another distortion of sacramental life comes in the adoration of the
Eucharist outside of the context of the act of communion:

Worship of the Eucharist. In the liturgy of the Mass we express our faith in
the real presence of Christ under the species of bread and wine by, among
other ways, genuflecting or bowing deeply as a sign of adoration of the Lord.
"The Catholic Church has always offered and still offers to the sacrament of
the Eucharist the cult of adoration, not only during Mass, but also outside
of it, reserving the consecrated hosts with the utmost care, exposing them
to the solemn veneration of the faithful, and carrying them in procession."
(CCC, 1378)

One can spend time in special "adoration chapels," whose whole purpose
is to allow the faithful to come into the presence of the Eucharist, to worship
it and meditate on it. For the Orthodox, while we always respect the reserved
sacrament (set aside for the communion of the sick), to remove the Eucharist
from the context of communion is nonsense. The Lord said for us to eat and
drink His flesh and blood (John 6:53–56). He said nothing about removing
them from that context.

The category of validity allows for ecclesiastical lines to be crossed, even if
there is no communion between ecclesial bodies. It allows Rome to recognize
"valid" sacraments even outside its own self-understanding of the Church (i.e.,
the Church is only the Roman Catholic Church):

Eastern Christians who are in fact separated in good faith from the Catholic Church, if they ask of their own accord and have the right dispositions, may be admitted to the sacraments of Penance, the Eucharist and the Anointing of the Sick. Further, Catholics may ask for these same sacraments from those non-Catholic ministers whose churches possess valid sacraments, as often as necessity or a genuine spiritual benefit recommends such a course and access to a Catholic priest is physically or morally impossible. (Vatican II, *Orientalium Ecclesiarium*, 1964)

For the Orthodox, communion and all the sacraments exist only within one ecclesiastical communion. That is, Orthodox Christians may only receive the sacraments from Orthodox clergy. Likewise, Orthodox clergy may only give the sacraments to Orthodox Christians. (In cases of emergency, non-Orthodox are welcome to convert in order to receive the sacraments.)

Sacramental validity also allows for the possibility of ordination itself having an existence outside the community of the Church, because ordination is "indelible":

As in the case of Baptism and Confirmation this share in Christ's office is granted once for all. The sacrament of Holy Orders, like the other two, confers an *indelible spiritual character* and cannot be repeated or conferred temporarily.

It is true that someone validly ordained can, for grave reasons, be discharged from the obligations and functions linked to ordination, or can be forbidden to exercise them; but he cannot become a layman again in the strict sense, because the character imprinted by ordination is for ever. The vocation and mission received on the day of his ordination mark him permanently. (CCC, 1582–83)

It is because of the indelible mark of Roman Catholic ordination theology that its doctrine of apostolic succession is truncated. All that is needed for apostolic succession for Rome is that there be proof that an ordination can be traced through a valid line of bishops back to the Apostles. For the Orthodox, however, that line is not enough. The apostolic faith and maintenance of communion within the Church are also required. Rome sees lines of "valid" bishops outside its own communion, but Orthodoxy recognizes no such thing.

For the Orthodox, ordination exists within and for the Church. If a clergyman leaves the Church, he is no longer a clergyman. Likewise, if he is removed from the ranks of the clergy by the Church, he is truly a layman once again.

Sacramental validity is what makes marriage annulment possible—one could be married for years and then discover a technicality which renders one not married. This possibility exists because the couple are regarded as the ministers of the sacrament, not the priest. Marriage is primarily understood as a legal contract. (Orthodoxy does have a kind of annulment, but not one based on intention or technicality—a man cannot marry his sister, for instance, even if he goes through the marriage rite with her. Therefore, such a "wedding" would be automatically invalid.)

The existence of Eastern Catholic rites which still use Orthodox practices—such as immediate chrismation/confirmation at baptism and the theology of the priest as the minister of the marriage sacrament—is a severe contradiction given the standard Latin practice. If an Eastern Catholic marriage is annulled, then does that mean that the priest (probably without knowing it) acted invalidly?

A NOTE OF CAUTION

Having said all this, we must add that it is critical for Orthodox Christians to note that twentieth- and twenty-first-century Roman Catholicism has seen a number of developments bringing some theologians closer to Orthodoxy and others further away. There is much in the *Ressourcement* (French, "going back to the sources") movement with its fresh emphasis on the Church Fathers that should encourage the Orthodox. At the same time, certain disturbing distortions occurred in some sectors of the Roman Catholic Church in the twentieth century, such as Liberation Theology, an attempt to wed church dogma with Marxist politics.

Because of these kinds of developments—as well as the ongoing problem of the gap between official Vatican teaching and what the average Roman Catholic personally believes or is taught from the pulpit—Orthodox believers should tread lightly in discussing theology with Roman Catholics. They may be closer to or further from Orthodoxy than what is officially taught by the Vatican. It is critical to discern what the person in front of you believes before launching into any sort of detailed refutation of Roman Catholic dogma and practice.

I also believe that much of modern Orthodox criticism of Roman Catholicism is based either on pre-twentieth-century models of Rome's thought or simply on mischaracterizations and oversimplifications of its theology and practice. In my opinion, many of the Orthodox writers of our time have borrowed heavily from Protestant polemics against Rome, which are often based either in exaggerations or misunderstandings of Rome's theology or are instead based on Protestant theology which is not consistent with Orthodoxy. Again, it is critical that we understand the theology of the person in front of us as well as our own.

THE GROUNDS OF UNION

In summary, in order for the Orthodox Church to accept sacramental communion with the Roman Catholic Church—that is, for Roman Catholics to be readmitted into the Orthodox Church—they must repudiate and reject (not merely brush aside or "theologize around") the following:

- Papal universal jurisdiction
- Papal infallibility
- Papal Petrine exclusivism (i.e., that only the pope is Peter's successor)
- Development of doctrine
- The *Filioque*
- Original sin understood as guilt transmitted via "propagation"
- The immaculate conception of Mary
- Absolute divine simplicity
- Merit and satisfaction soteriology
- Purgatory and indulgences
- Created grace

Roman Catholics would have to accept and fully confess:

- The authority of Ecumenical Councils over the pope
- The essence/energies distinction

Roman Catholics would have to restore Orthodox practices (already present for Eastern Catholics):

- Reconnect confirmation/chrismation to baptism rather than delaying it
- Give Holy Communion to all church members, including infants

In other words, what the Orthodox expect of Roman Catholics is that they become Orthodox again, that they return to the ancient Orthodox faith of the pre-Schism West. They would not have to give up their ancient traditions of worship (though they would probably want to turn the clock back on the liturgical revolution of Vatican II).

Three

The Magisterial Reformation

THE END OF ROMAN CATHOLIC EUROPE

Unless I am convinced by proofs from Scriptures or by plain and clear reasons and arguments, I can and will not retract, for it is neither safe nor wise to do anything against conscience. Here I stand. I can do no other. God help me. Amen.

> (Martin Luther, 1521)

God preordained, for His own glory and the display of His attributes of mercy and justice, a part of the human race, without any merit of their own, to eternal salvation, and another part, in just punishment of their sin, to eternal damnation.

> (John Calvin, *Institutes of the Christian Religion,* 1536)

From the gospel we learn that the doctrines and traditions of men are of no use to salvation.

> (Huldrych Zwingli, *The Sixty-Seven Articles,* 1523)

The iconic moment that touched off the sixteenth-century Protestant Reformation was the nailing of ninety-five theses to the door of the church in Wittenberg on October 31, 1517, by Martin Luther, an Augustinian monk who had become desperate for the reform of the Roman Catholic Church. He never had any intention of forming a new denomination, but his insistence on the abolition of indulgences and their sale, as well as his affirmation of the supremacy of the Bible over the church hierarchy, provoked his excommunication by Rome in 1520.

Historians call the first wave of the Reformation the "Magisterial Reformation," since it had the backing of the civil authorities (the magistracy), particularly in what is now Germany. These first Reformers had no problem with working together with the secular authorities for the good of their churches. With the help of this magistracy, the solid hold of Rome over the religious unity of Western Europe came to an end.

The denominations produced by the Magisterial Reformation, all of which differ from one another on major points of doctrine and practice, include: Lutherans (including the various forms of Pietism), the Reformed churches (both Calvinists and Zwinglians, including Presbyterians, Puritans, Congregationalists, and Dutch Reformed), and Anglicans (including Episcopalians). Although historically later (18th c.), Methodists and Wesleyans, which branched from the Anglicans, may be classified with these groups.

THE FIVE SOLAS

Although the Reformation quickly splintered along doctrinal lines, there were five "solas" (Latin for "alone") that characterized most Reformation theology: *sola scriptura* ("Scripture alone"), *sola fide* ("Faith alone"), *sola gratia* ("Grace alone"), *solus Christus* ("Christ alone"), and *soli Deo gloria* ("To God alone be glory"). These five doctrinal positions are the pillars of the Protestant Reformation. In one form or another, they continue to be believed by all the denominations of the Magisterial Reformation and deeply influence all Protestant churches. In some ways, Orthodoxy agrees with all of these "solas," but also differs from them in important ways.

Sola Scriptura

In its basic form, *sola scriptura* means "by Scripture alone." At the beginning of the Reformation, it did not mean a total abandonment of all church tradition, but simply attempted to elevate Scripture to the highest and most central point of Christian life. It was not long, however, before its at least implicit divorce from tradition—most especially hermeneutical tradition, that is, how one interprets the Bible—would lead to various doctrinal revolutions.

Under Luther, *sola scriptura* was especially defined in anticlerical terms:

I have the right to believe freely, to be a slave to no man's authority, to confess what appears to be true whether it is proved or disproved, whether it is spoken by Catholic or by heretic. . . . In matters of faith I think that neither counsel nor Pope nor any man has the power over my conscience. And where they disagree with Scripture, I deny Pope and council and all. A simple layman armed with Scripture is greater than the mightiest Pope without it. (from his defense at the Diet of Worms in 1521)

Luther's words have to be understood specifically in terms of their contemporary context: The Reformers were seeking to address the abuses of Rome, most especially what they regarded as a vast accumulation of un-Christian doctrines and practices in the name of "Tradition." Yet the new Reformation principle of authority—which is predicated upon the "priesthood of all believers" (as expressed above by Luther)—bears within it the seeds of a whole new form of Christianity, especially now that Protestants are no longer actively confronting Rome (except in occasional rhetoric from the pulpit).

All this raises the question of who has the authority to interpret the Bible. Under the Swiss Reformer Hudlrych Zwingli, *sola scriptura* came to mean much more than before, going so far as to claim that the Bible is the single, exclusive source of all Christian doctrine and practice (which led Zwingli to abolish every Christian ritual he couldn't find in the Bible). This view is the position of most Protestant denominations today, who have largely abandoned the notion of tradition entirely. Some differ on whether what is not mentioned in Scripture is forbidden or to be left to local custom to decide. Either way, all idea of authoritative tradition is rejected.

Orthodoxy, by contrast, holds the Scripture in extremely high regard, but holds it to be a book written by the Church, for the Church, and within the Church. As such, reading it correctly requires the light of Holy Tradition, the faith given to the Apostles by Christ via oral teaching and preserved within the Church.

Sola scriptura is the most important defining and distinctive doctrine for all of Protestantism. With this principle, any doctrine or practice may be "proven" from Scripture, depending on how one reads it. On this principle all the Protestant denominations were founded. Without it, the question of authority comes into play, and the believer finds that he has to be obedient to someone else's interpretation of the Scripture.

Most Protestant denominations believe that all Christian doctrine may be derived from Scripture by means of the "plain sense" of the text, which is derived from the use of reason, history, and textual study. Its purpose is to find out what the writers "really meant" when they penned the books of the Bible. With this in mind, most *sola scriptura* believers regard their own interpretation of the Bible as right, while those who differ are wrong. Those who are wrong are so usually because of alleged flaws in their logic.

A notable exception is classical Anglicanism/Episcopalianism, which since the late sixteenth century has claimed to base its doctrine on three pillars: scripture, reason, and tradition. (Modern Anglicanism has all but rejected all three in any meaningful sense. One can now teach and do almost anything at all and remain an Anglican in good standing.)

The Orthodox have multiple objections to the doctrine of *sola scriptura*, on the grounds of clear reason, on practical grounds, and also from church history and tradition. First, *sola scriptura* fails its own test, since such an idea is found nowhere in the Bible. It is true that the Bible speaks very highly of the value of Scripture (e.g., 2 Tim. 3:16), but never does it say that it is exclusively authoritative. Ironically, the Bible describes the Church (not itself) as the "pillar and ground of the truth" (1 Tim. 3:15).

St. Paul also notably commands believers in Thessalonica not merely to read the Bible, but to "stand fast and hold the traditions which you were taught, whether by word [of mouth] or our epistle" (2 Thess. 2:15). That is, Paul expects them to hold to church tradition, whether it is written (Scripture) or passed on by oral teaching. Readers of the Protestant New International Version (NIV) translation will miss this, because the NIV translates the Greek word *paradosis* ("tradition") as "teaching" when it is used in a good light but as "tradition" when used negatively. This approach distorts what the Bible actually says, distinguishing between two different kinds of *paradosis*, that of man and that of God.

Another logical problem with making the Bible an exclusively authoritative source is that its very design does not lend itself to such usage. There is no systematic theology or catechism in the Bible. There is also no manual in it on important matters such as how one is to worship God. The Bible is rather a collection of documents of various genres written for various purposes: history, poetry, pastoral teaching, prophecy, and apocalypse. But nowhere do we find in it an exhaustive manual on Christian life.

A number of practical problems are introduced by *sola scriptura*, as well. The old Roman Catholic characterization of *sola scriptura*, "every man his own pope," is apt in Orthodoxy's eyes as well (though of course we object to the idea of an infallible papacy!). Because every believer becomes authoritative in interpreting the Scripture, we have to ask how we are to defend against heresy. Indeed, what is heresy? How can Protestants object to an infallible papacy while teaching their own personal infallibility?

What's telling about this approach to Scripture, rejecting church tradition, is that Protestants tend to interpret according to traditions, anyway. There is a certain consistency among most Presbyterians, Lutherans, and so on, because they are following their own teachers in the faith. Thus, they violate their own principle every time a sermon or Bible class is taught, because in all those cases, a teacher is presuming to tell someone else how to read the Bible.

In terms of the actual working out of the interpretation of Scripture, most *sola scriptura* believers will say that the Holy Spirit guides the individual reader. But if that is true, why is there such conflict within Protestantism over what the Bible means? If the text is clear on its own, why has this hermeneutic (interpretive principle) not united all Protestants together but instead continues to fracture them? How does the honest, but confused, believer decide between all the different people who insist that "the Bible clearly says" various things, yet all disagree with each other? How does he decide whose claim on the Holy Spirit's guidance is the valid one?

Some will admit that parts of the Bible are less clear and that we should therefore interpret the unclear passages by means of the clear ones. But who decides which passages are going to be defined as "clear"? Again, we are left with the problem of authority.

Others with a high view of the academic world will turn to biblical scholars, using historical-critical methods of exegesis, to make clear what is not. Yet anyone even cursorily familiar with the world of academic biblical scholarship will easily attest to its utter chaos and division. Unity by this method remains elusive. And what happens when the next manuscript variant or archaeological find is uncovered? Are we to revolutionize our whole understanding of the Christian faith? Those who watch the media around Christmas and Easter with any diligence note that they somehow always come up with some new startling discovery from the ancient world that is supposed to make believers question everything they've always affirmed.

There are also several major historical problems with *sola scriptura*. Most notably, this doctrine is absent from the writings of the Church Fathers. Whether one considers them authoritative or not, what it means is that, if the Apostles taught *sola scriptura* (despite leaving it out of the New Testament), their disciples and those who followed them don't seem to have learned that lesson.

At the same time, *sola scriptura* would have been a practical impossibility for the early Church. After the Resurrection of Jesus, it was roughly twenty to forty years before the New Testament began to be written (some scholars put Paul's 1 Thessalonians as the first book to be written, while others give that distinction to Galatians). The last of the New Testament documents, St. John's Revelation (or Apocalypse), was probably written in AD 95. Christians therefore had to wait about sixty years before it was finished.

Yet in the year 95, the Apostle John did not finish Revelation, send his manuscript off to a publisher along with the rest of the New Testament books, and get them published for distribution in the Church. These various books circulated separately for a long time, being read in church services and quoted by later Christian writers, often alongside other books that we would not now recognize as Scripture. It was not until the year 367 that the list of the twenty-seven New Testament books as we now know them came to be produced. In that year, St. Athanasius the Great, the Patriarch of Alexandria (and the hero of the First Ecumenical Council in Nicea in 325), wrote a letter to his churches instructing them on which books were to be considered canonical. From the time of the founding of the Church with the descent of the Holy Spirit at Pentecost to when Christians could finally point to a canon for the New Testament was more than three hundred years. The question, "What does the Bible say?" could not be asked, because the question, "What is the Bible?" had not yet been answered.

Ironically for the Reformers, "What is the Bible?" came to be asked again in the sixteenth century, because they proceeded to edit the actual canon to suit their own tastes, removing books from the Old Testament that had been considered canonical for centuries (e.g., the Maccabees, Tobit, etc.). What good is *sola scriptura* when you can change what constitutes Scripture? And where in the canon is the canon itself defined?

For the Orthodox, the Bible—its contents, canonization, and interpretation—have always been a matter for the church community. Authority was given by Christ to His Church, and so the Church used that authority to write the Bible and to compile and canonize it. The Church still uses that authority to interpret it.

Sola Fide

The doctrine of *sola fide* teaches that justification comes by faith alone. In classical Protestant doctrine, justification is being "declared righteous" ("imputed" righteousness) by God. The doctrine of imputed righteousness is in contrast with the Roman Catholic teaching of infused righteousness (that God puts righteousness into the believer and it becomes part of him). To have righteousness imputed is to be reckoned righteous by God, but without any actual righteousness being in the person. It is a change in legal status, but not in personal holiness, not even a change effected by grace. In this, the doctrine directly descends from Roman Catholic theology with its emphasis on legal status.

Faith alone is specifically contrasted with good works. That is, good works have nothing to do with salvation other than being a symptom or sign of true faith. True faith will always lead to two things: justification and good works. Luther described this doctrine as being the "doctrine by which the church stands or falls."

Sola fide finds its clearest formulations in both the *Augsburg Confession* and the *Westminster Confession of Faith*, which are authoritative doctrinal statements for Lutheran and Reformed Christians, respectively:

> Our churches by common consent . . . teach that men cannot be justified
> before God by their own strength, merits, or works, but are freely justified
> for Christ's sake, through faith, when they believe that they are received into

favor, and that their sins are forgiven for Christ's sake, who, by His death, has made satisfaction for our sins. This faith God imputes for righteousness in His sight. (*Augsburg Confession*, 1530)

Those whom God effectually calls, He also freely justifies; not by infusing righteousness into them, but by pardoning their sins, and by accounting and accepting their persons as righteous; not for any thing wrought in them, or done by them, but for Christ's sake alone; nor by imputing faith itself, the act of believing, or any other evangelical obedience to them, as their righteousness; but by imputing the obedience and satisfaction of Christ unto them, they receiving and resting on Him and His righteousness by faith; which faith they have not of themselves, it is the gift of God. (*Westminster Confession of Faith*, 1647)

Sola fide was formulated primarily in response to the Roman Catholic insistence on good works (and the whole system of merit, satisfaction, purgatory, and indulgences), which was interpreted by Luther as trying to earn one's way to heaven. (That is not what Roman Catholicism officially taught, but it was a popular understanding of Catholic doctrine in the sixteenth century and was likely preached by those who sold indulgences.) From this comes the almost universal Protestant tradition about Roman Catholicism, that it teaches "works righteousness," that Catholics believe that they "earn" salvation. The Reformers also viewed monasticism in this way, that it is an attempt to earn salvation.

Luther was so insistent on this formulation that, when he was translating Romans 3:28 into German, he added the German word *allein* ("alone"), so that the verse would read: "Therefore we conclude that a man is justified by faith *alone* without the deeds of the law." But the word *alone* is not present in the Greek text. Luther was also so vexed by the apparent opposition to his doctrine in the Epistle of James that he wrote, "St. James' Epistle is really an epistle of straw . . . for it has nothing of the nature of the Gospel about it." (He also questioned the authority of Jude, Hebrews, and Revelation.) Ironically, the only place "faith alone" (or sometimes "faith only") appears as a phrase in the New Testament is in James 2:24: "You see then that a man is justified by works, and not by faith only." James also says, in 2:17: "Thus also faith by itself, if it does not have works, is dead." (While Luther did want to omit James from his canon, he eventually chose to leave it in place.)

In later Protestantism, *sola fide* came to be understood as meaning simple belief or agreement with certain doctrinal propositions, such that salvation depends not on faithfulness but on a one-time assent.

Orthodoxy, by contrast, teaches with the Scripture that it is by grace through faith that we are saved, and not of works (Eph. 2:8–9). Where Orthodoxy differs from the doctrine of *sola fide* is in its understanding of faith, works, and justification. Faith for the Orthodox Christian includes good works, not because they earn salvation, but because they are a form of cooperation with divine grace, which does the work of transformation. Justification for the Orthodox is being made really righteous, not simply declared so. This is only possible by means of the ongoing presence of God in a person.

The concept of good works in the Scripture is misunderstood by Luther as being equal to "the works of the law," that is, the Mosaic Law. Yet while St. Paul preaches against the value of the Jewish law for salvation, he nowhere preaches against good works themselves. Luther's error was in conflating the two. "The works of the law" that do not help us are Jewish tradition, but the good "works" without which faith is "dead" (James 2:17–26) constitute the righteous life of the believer. Even then, these good works do not *in themselves* accomplish anything. It is God's grace that makes the transformation possible. It is our life of faith and good works that is our cooperation with divine grace, the free gift of God. This is called *synergy*. God calls us not merely to believe or trust Him, but to "be perfect" (Matt. 5:48).

Sola Gratia

The teaching of *sola gratia* ("by grace alone") is that it is only God's grace that accomplishes salvation. No act of man contributes to salvation in any way. This doctrine is closely associated with *sola fide*, as faith is what activates saving grace. *Sola gratia* believers usually state their doctrine in terms opposed to Pelagianism (the doctrine that man may achieve salvation without divine help, because he is not subject to original/ancestral sin, i.e., his will remains unimpaired by the Fall). Anyone suggesting that man has any substantial role in his salvation is usually accused of being either Pelagian or semi-Pelagian.

The most extreme form of this doctrine is held by classical Calvinism, which holds that man has absolutely no role in his salvation, not even assent. That is, God saves you whether you want it or not. He also damns you whether you want it or not. These two actions together are called double predestination. In this case, both faith and grace are gifts from God and do not involve man's will in any way. Grace is often termed "irresistible." Most *sola gratia* believers are not this extreme, however; they believe that man must at least assent to salvation at some point, even if only once.

Orthodox can agree with *sola gratia* if it is understood to mean that it is God's grace that does the actual transforming work of salvation. However, Orthodoxy believes in *synergy*, that God and man are co-workers (2 Cor. 6:1), that man must "work out [his] own salvation with fear and trembling" (Phil. 2:12).

One of the principal problems with *sola gratia* is an inheritance from Roman Catholicism, namely, that grace is something other than God Himself. In Reformation theology, grace is "unmerited favor." For Orthodoxy, grace is uncreated—that is, grace is God, His actual presence and activity. If grace is merely "favor," then union with God (*theosis*) is precluded. The distance from God found in Roman Catholic theology is retained in Protestantism.

Solus Christus

Solus Christus, the teaching that "Christ alone" is the means of salvation, was formulated in response to the strongly mediatorial understanding of sixteenth-century Roman Catholic clergy. The fear is that a fallible human being would presume to stand between a believer and God. This interpretation of Roman Catholic doctrine comes from its teachings on the pope as the vicar of Christ on earth, the notion of meritorious works done by the saints, and most especially the idea that the pope can dispense those merits as he pleases. Although Roman Catholic teaching often emphasizes the mediatorial role of clergy, in our own day, at least, it is not as extreme as the Reformers characterized it. This Reformation attitude is a sort of Donatism, but instead of a denial of the efficacy of sacraments from a particular wicked priest, it is a denial of the priesthood altogether.

In the sense that the Reformers usually meant it, that salvation is possible only in and through Christ, *solus Christus* is acceptable to Orthodoxy. However, the accompanying rejection of the clerical role, most especially in serving the sacraments, which some Reformers interpreted this doctrine to include is not acceptable to Orthodoxy. They emphasized the "priesthood of all believers," implying that there is no sacerdotal priesthood. Orthodoxy also believes in the priesthood of all believers, but not in the eldership (the meaning of the presbyterate) of all believers. We also note that ancient Israel had a similar notion for all believers, yet retained a sacrificial priesthood to conduct the Temple worship.

Protestants also tend to reject the intercession of saints, since "Christ alone" has anything to do with salvation. The Orthodox Church has never emphasized the clergy as mediators, because there is only one Mediator between God and man, Jesus Christ (1 Tim. 2:5). The clergy are, however, intercessors, just as the saints are. Clergy also have a role to play in salvation as the ministers of the sacraments, but it is not an absolute role, since God may save someone in spite of the wickedness of a priest.

Soli Deo Gloria

Soli Deo gloria is the teaching that to God alone is due glory. This doctrine is a direct rejection of the veneration of saints and other holy objects or persons. It is a reaction to the ostentatious earthly glory of sixteenth-century Roman Catholicism. In some ways, *soli Deo gloria* may be regarded as redundant with *solus Christus*, since it emphasizes salvation as being only from God; but it adds the idea that human beings should not seek out their own glory (in other words, it preaches humility).

Orthodoxy agrees with the essence of this doctrine, that God alone is worthy of our worship. However, it is a rejection of His Incarnation and of His work in human beings in history to deny honor to those people and places. Veneration is given to saints only because of the work of Christ in them. It in no way detracts from the worship due to God alone. We should of course never seek our own glory, but there is nothing wrong with showing respect and veneration to God's saints, who show forth His glory.

Therefore, *soli Deo gloria*, while attempting to preserve the exclusive worship of God, in fact detracts from His saving work in His creation. Underneath it is the spiritual attitude that there can be no true union between the Uncreated and the created, only a bestowal of "favor." When applied to Christology, this is crypto-Nestorianism.

In its emphasis on humility, *soli Deo gloria* has been used as a way of giving thanks to God for a particular work of art. The great Baroque composer Johann Sebastian Bach, for instance, wrote "SDG" on many of his musical manuscripts. Athletes ?

MAGISTERIAL REFORMATION DENOMINATIONS

Aside from the general inheritance of the five *solas* from the Magisterial Reformation, the various denominations that arose from the first wave of the Reformation also have their own distinctives.

Lutheranism

Views of scriptural interpretation now vary within Lutheranism. Some Lutherans follow the seventeenth-century approach, which emphasized biblical inerrancy (the teaching that the Scripture is correct and totally consistent in absolutely every detail, no matter how minor). Others are influenced by eighteenth-century rationalism, which questioned the authority of the Bible itself. The nineteenth century saw for Lutherans a renewed interest in confessionalism, i.e., placing authority in early Lutheran texts (e.g., the *Book of Concord*, the *Augsburg Confession*, etc.)—essentially an appeal to Lutheran tradition.

Orthodoxy regards all Scripture as being properly interpreted only within the Orthodox Church. There is no need for the doctrine of inerrancy, because it does not matter whether the Bible is correct on trivial issues, such as the precise distance between towns. Rationalism also has no place within Orthodoxy, because human reason is notoriously fallible. Orthodoxy lauds any call to return to tradition, but in the case of Lutheran confessionalism, it's a tradition that is divorced from Holy Tradition and therefore lacking and incorrect in various ways.

Lutherans in general regard the contents of Scripture as being divided into Law and Gospel. Law is regarded as obedience to God's ethical commands, while Gospel is what grants forgiveness of sins and salvation. As such, only Gospel is truly necessary for salvation (see above on *sola fide* and *sola gratia*), but the Law can help bring us to salvation in that it shows us our sins. Orthodoxy accepts no such division of the Scriptures and regards them all as being for our salvation.

Aside from questions of scriptural interpretation, Lutherans only recognize two sacraments, baptism and Holy Communion (although Luther himself regarded confession as a sacrament at one point, but in some sense as part of baptism). They vary as to whether anything "real" happens in the sacraments, depending largely on their divisions according to the above-described hermeneutical camps.

Lutherans traditionally believe that baptism is a saving work of God (though they differ on what that means), and they administer it to infants.

For Lutherans, Holy Communion traditionally includes a belief in the real presence of Christ, but not in terms of the bread and wine being changed into the Body and Blood of Christ. (This is in opposition to the Roman Catholic doctrine of transubstantiation, which teaches that the "substance" of the bread and wine are changed, but that their "accidents" remain, which is why they still look the same.) Rather, Luther believed that Christ's Body and Blood were "in, with and under" the bread and wine. This view is sometimes called consubstantiation, but that term is often rejected by Lutherans as too philosophical. ~~Seems~~ like a mixed garbage

Orthodoxy has always rejected all such speculation or definition and says simply that the bread and wine become Christ's Body and Blood. How this happens, whether the bread and wine are still in some way present, and so forth, are not treated as dogmatic concerns. Luther's "in, with and under" language may also be understood in an essentially Orthodox manner.

The major Lutheran denominations in America are the Evangelical Lutheran Church in America (ELCA), Lutheran Church—Missouri Synod (LCMS), and Wisconsin Evangelical Lutheran Synod (WELS).

In general, the ELCA, the largest, is regarded as the most liberal. It ordains women and is the least confessional of all Lutheran groups. The LCMS and WELS are much more conservative, do not ordain women, and are more likely to be confessional. There are many smaller Lutheran denominations in the United States, including the newly formed (as of 2010) North American Lutheran Church (NALC), which is a breakaway body from the ELCA and describes itself as representing the "theological center" of Lutheranism in America.

The more conservative denominations are more likely to have a liturgical type of worship. This worship is relatively informal in comparison with the more catholic traditions, with a higher emphasis on preaching than in most liturgical traditions. Many Lutheran denominations, such as Swedish Lutherans, maintain a theology of apostolic succession for their bishops. Not all Lutherans have bishops.

In other countries, Lutherans are often simply called "Evangelicals," which has a meaning different from its meaning within the US. In Germany, *Evangelische* also refers to Protestantism in general.

The Reformed Churches

Calvinism, named for the teachings of John Calvin (a lawyer from Geneva), strongly influenced a number of Protestant groups. Calvinism is a tightly argued, highly rationalistic view of the relationship between God's foreknowledge, His sovereignty, and man's free will. While there is much more to Calvin's teachings than his views on predestination, Calvinism itself is usually defined by the set of doctrines called "five point Calvinism."

These five points are (1) total depravity (the Fall of mankind utterly obliterated any goodness in man, rendering him incapable of choosing God), (2) unconditional election (God's choice to save certain people is not based on anything they have done and was made before even creation itself), (3) limited atonement (Christ's substitutionary sacrifice on the cross is only salvific for the elect), (4) irresistible grace (when God chooses to save someone, that one has no choice but to be saved; free will is in no way involved), and (5) the perseverance of the saints (once God has saved someone, that one will never fall away; those who do fall away were never really saved). The first initials of these doctrines form the acronym TULIP, which is a useful mnemonic device for remembering them all.

Implied in these points (and taught by Calvin) is the corollary that if man has no choice in being saved and if God only saves some, then that means that He has deliberately chosen some for damnation—whether anyone desires it or not, whether they want to follow God or not. This view is called double predestination, and it has its origins in some of the errors of St. Augustine. In essence, before all time, God wrote two lists, of the elect and the reprobate, and there is nothing anyone can do to get his name moved from one list to the other.

Orthodoxy rejects all five points, which are mainly predicated on a denial of man's free will. As the famous Protestant preacher John Wesley once pointed out, what would be the point of all of Christ's and the Apostles' preaching, if those to whom they were preaching had no choice about whether to be saved? For Orthodoxy, although man's will is infected by the Fall, his ability to choose God has not been destroyed but only impaired.

Orthodox Christians see Calvinism as truly monstrous, most especially because it depicts a God who arbitrarily saves some people and damns others. Such a "God" is not the God of a loving relationship, the gentle Christ who woos His bride, the Church. Rather, this is a capricious, erratic, vengeful "God," who saves some men and damns others for no apparent reason. Further, Christ did not die on the cross as a substitute for mankind's punishment, but rather so that He might enter into death and destroy its power.

Calvin is consistent in his low view of man's nature and his commitment to double predestination, and he therefore uses strong language to express it:

> We are all made of mud, and as this mud is not just on the hem of our gown, or on the sole of our boots, or in our shoes. We are full of it, we are nothing but mud and filth both inside and outside. (Calvin's *Institutes of the Christian Religion*)

> We may rest assured that God would never have suffered any infants to be slain except those who were already damned and predestined for eternal death. (*ibid.*)

Calvinists also subscribe to the eucharistic theory of receptionism, that is, that the benefits of the Body and Blood of Christ are only present if the believer receives the Eucharist by faith. But there is nothing actually there in the bread and the wine, and Christ is fed on by faith only and not with the mouth. This approach contrasts with Orthodoxy, which believes that Christ's Body and Blood are objectively what is being received by the communicant, which is why receiving can be to his damnation: "For he who eats and drinks in an unworthy manner eats and drinks judgment to himself, not discerning the Lord's body" (1 Cor. 11:29).

Calvin himself also taught theocracy, subjecting the government to the church, which led to the burning of one heretic in Geneva; but this is no longer a part of most Calvinist belief. In fairness, it should be noted that the one heretic who was burned, Miguel de Serveto, was strongly heretical, rejecting the doctrine of the Trinity and calling for the violent overthrow of both Catholic and Protestant societies. Also, his execution occurred in 1533, before Calvin himself had much influence in the Geneva government. Nevertheless, the Orthodox do not teach theocracy nor that heretics ought to be burned.

Among Calvinists, Presbyterians hold to a form of church government in which regional governance is by a council of presbyters (pastors), rather than bishops.

Most Reformed denominations no longer hold strictly to five-point Calvinism, particularly the element of the predestination of both the elect and the damned. Many of these denominations will also ordain women. The United Church of Christ in particular has embraced a highly liberal approach to theology and morality.

Zwinglianism, based in the teachings of Huldrych Zwingli of Switzerland (who predated Calvin in the Swiss Reformation), is not represented by any specific denomination in our own time. Nevertheless, Zwingli profoundly influenced a number of Reformed groups, including those otherwise regarded as Calvinist. There is no agreed-upon definition of "Zwinglianism" *per se*, but Zwingli is most associated with teaching that the sacraments are purely symbolic.

Zwingli and Luther agreed on a number of important points, but diverged on others, most especially the Eucharist, which Zwingli regarded as being solely symbolic—not a present reality, but merely a sign of God's past acts. He also regarded the teaching that baptism actually accomplished anything salvific as superstition. He had an essentially dualistic view of the universe, that material reality had no part to play in salvation.

Zwingli's version of *sola scriptura* was more radical than Luther's. Instead of its being merely the highest authority for Christian life, Zwingli taught that Scripture had exclusive, independent authority. He was largely responsible for the unmooring of Scripture from all sense of tradition. Scripture was to be read in exclusive isolation and all meaning derived from that method. (He nevertheless selectively quoted from the Church Fathers in an attempt to prove that his views were not exclusively his own.)

Reformed churches previously worshiped in a liturgical manner, following the Lutherans, but now virtually all of them have abandoned liturgical worship in favor of the worship styles inherited from the revivalist movements of the nineteenth and twentieth centuries. The primary focus in the worship of these churches is the sermon.

Arminianism was a reaction to the deterministic logic of Calvinism, first elucidated in the seventeenth century by Jacobus Arminius. Arminius, unlike Calvin, taught that man's free will was real and effective in salvation or damnation, and in this he is in agreement with Orthodoxy. He also taught that any predestination on the part of God is according to God's foreknowledge—that is, because God knew that certain people would freely choose to be saved, He acted in accordance with that choice. This is also essentially Orthodox.

However, like Calvin, Arminius taught that man is totally depraved, and so all choosing of God is the result of the direct action of divine grace. Like most Western theologians, he also taught the "satisfaction of divine justice" theory of salvation. Like Orthodoxy, however, he taught that it was possible to fall away from God. Unlike Orthodoxy, he may have believed that it was impossible to return from such apostasy.

Arminianism in one form or another has profoundly influenced much of modern Protestantism.

The major Reformed denominations in America are the Presbyterian Church USA (PCUSA), Presbyterian Church in America (PCA), Reformed Church in America ("Dutch Reformed"), Christian Reformed Church ("Dutch Reformed"), and the United Church of Christ (UCC).

Anglicanism and its Heirs

Anglicanism, represented in America primarily by the **Episcopal Church USA (ECUSA)**, originated in a sixteenth-century schism from the Roman Catholic Church in England. The schism occurred not over doctrine, but over politics—mainly the pope's refusal to grant King Henry VIII a divorce so he could remarry. A disavowal of the pope's powers over the church naturally soon followed, along with an affirmation that the monarch of England was the "Supreme Governor" of the church there, outranking even the Archbishop of Canterbury. (Ironically, Henry had received the title Defender of the Faith from the pope before the schism, in reward for a writing by the king defending the sacraments and the supremacy of the pope against Martin Luther.)

Immediately after the schism from Rome in the 1530s, Anglican theology remained virtually unchanged from its Roman Catholic origins. Soon, however, it began to vacillate between the conservative theology of Rome and the more radical theology of the Reformers on the continent. This vacillation often followed changes in the ecclesiastical sympathies of whoever occupied the English throne. By the late seventeenth century, the Church of England attempted to form what it called a *via media*, that is, a "middle way" between Catholicism and Protestantism (though it was strongly Calvinistic until around 1660, owing to Queen Elizabeth I's church being dominated by men from Zurich after she officially switched England's religion back to Protestantism in 1559). Despite the desire for a *via media*, however, Anglicanism eventually drifted more and more toward Protestantism while retaining the outward forms of Rome's liturgical worship.

With the strong influence of Calvinism on Anglicanism, Britain saw the rise of the Puritans, Presbyterians, Separatists, and Congregationalists, many of whom were persecuted in England and headed for America (the Pilgrims of the Plymouth colony in Massachusetts among them).

In our own time, conservative, "catholic" Anglicanism mainly exists only in the Global South, with small pockets in the North, usually calling themselves "Anglo-Catholics," whose theology is in some respects quite close to Orthodoxy. The majority of Anglicans and Episcopalians in the Global North are highly liberal, however. They not only ordain women and openly practicing homosexuals, but they often may be found denying central truths common to almost all other Christians, such as the divinity of Jesus, the Virgin Birth, and the reality of the Resurrection. Many among the more liberal wing will often even incorporate non-Christian elements into their worship, such as paganism, witchcraft, and Buddhism. (I was once particularly grieved at seeing a statue of Buddha in the Episcopal chapel on the ancient holy island of Iona in Scotland, directly facing an Orthodox icon of the Resurrection.) Because of this theological chaos, a number of more conservative parishes and whole dioceses have broken away from their ecclesiastical provinces and are aligning themselves with Global South provinces, which are even now on the brink of excommunicating the Global North provinces.

Given this situation, the differences that Orthodox in America and Europe have with most Anglicans they may meet are so numerous that it may be almost impossible to find any common ground. This extreme liberalism in Anglicanism is of only relatively recent development, however, beginning in the twentieth century. Before that time, there were actually ongoing talks about establishing communion between Anglicanism and the Orthodox Church. As the Anglican and Episcopal churches have slid further into theological liberalism, their numbers have drastically fallen, and a number of their clergy and faithful have become either Roman Catholic or Orthodox. Even some Anglo-Catholics have gone in this direction, including one bishop who became an Orthodox priest, my friend Fr. Alban (formerly Robert) Waggener in Lynchburg, Virginia.

Methodists began as an eighteenth-century movement within the Anglican Church, but eventually broke off to form a new denomination, originally called Methodist Episcopalians. The brothers John and Charles Wesley, the movement's founders, along with their followers, earned the nickname Methodist due to espousing a "method" of Christian life, including ascetical elements. The Wesleys were clergy of the Church of England, but their followers eventually broke away from Anglicanism, much to the Wesleys' chagrin. The Wesleys read the Orthodox Fathers of the East and derived some theology from them, including the notion of "total sanctification," which is similar to the Orthodox doctrine of *theosis*.

Like most mainline denominations, modern Methodism has moved away from the Wesleys' emphasis on personal salvation and toward an emphasis on social justice, also referred to as the *social gospel*. There is also a great deal of theological liberalism in Methodism, and the largest Methodist denomination in the United States, the United Methodist Church, was founded explicitly on an agreement to accept doctrinal pluralism.

Most Methodists ordain women (including as bishops) and generally subscribe to a purely symbolic view of the Eucharist. Like most of the churches of the Magisterial Reformation, they will baptize infants, though they do not have any strong sacramental theology attached to the act.

The **Wesleyans** (formerly called "Wesleyan Methodists") are essentially an offshoot of Methodism, though because they came out of the Holiness Movement, their theology remains more focused on personal salvation rather than social justice, following more closely the theology of the Wesley brothers. (Three volumes were recently published by St. Vladimir's Seminary Press comparing Orthodox and Wesleyan theology: *Orthodox and Wesleyan Spirituality*, *Orthodox and Wesleyan Scriptural Understanding and Practice*, and *Orthodox and Wesleyan Ecclesiology*.)

The major Methodist and Wesleyan denominations in America are the United Methodist Church, the Free Methodist Church (originally so named because you didn't have to pay for your seat!), the African Methodist Episcopal Church, the African Methodist Episcopal Zion Church, and the Wesleyan Church.

COMMON GROUND

Almost as soon as it had begun, the Protestant Reformation immediately began to divide into factions, all with differences on major issues of theology. The major sticking points were the issues of (1) whether free will had any role to play in man's salvation and (2) the true nature of the Eucharist. Even Luther himself, who is generally regarded as the father of the Reformation, altered his own theology as time went by.

In the generation after Luther, when several theological factions of Protestants had formed, some empowered by the state through either government sponsorship or outright theocracy, a theological correspondence began between several second-generation Lutheran theologians in Tübingen and the Ecumenical Patriarch of Constantinople, whose patriarchate had been under Ottoman rule for over a century.

The Lutherans, it seemed, had hoped to find in the Orthodox East an ally against their common enemy in the Roman papacy. Because the Reformers understood themselves not as innovating in doctrine but rather as purging the Western church of innovations, and because it was believed that the East had retained its purity against the papacy, these Lutherans probably believed they would discover that the Orthodox were in fact theologically Lutheran.

Over the course of eight years, letters were exchanged between Tübingen and Patriarch Jeremiah, discussing theology and practice within their respective communions. To the Lutherans' dismay, however, the patriarch eventually asked them to stop writing to him about theological matters, because it was clear to him that they would never be able to agree. There was, of course, much that they had in common, but there was much on which they differed, namely: the role of tradition, monasticism, the procession of the Holy Spirit (the Lutherans confessed the *Filioque*), free will, predestination, justification, the number of sacraments, how and when baptism and chrismation were to be administered, the nature of the Eucharist, whether the Church and the Ecumenical Councils could be infallible, the veneration of saints and their icons and relics, and the celebration of feast days.

In short, while there was common ground on a number of subjects—in those areas where the Lutherans really had turned the clock back on Roman Catholic innovations—there remained two types of substantial disagreement: the theological inheritance from Rome, and innovations on the part of the Reformers. In particular, the Reformers continued, with Rome, to look at salvation primarily in legal terms rather than in terms of the personal transformation and communion with God Orthodoxy had preached since the first century. Much of this follows from the Western expansion on the errors of St. Augustine, usually labeled Augustinianism (which should be distinguished from St. Augustine himself).

The linchpin of all the innovations of Protestantism was the doctrine of *sola scriptura*. Because the Reformers believed they could read the Bible and derive all theology from it without reliance on authoritative Church tradition, they were bound to make mistakes. Every person brings a set of biases and presuppositions to reading the Bible. The only way to make sure you read it correctly is to make sure that you're functioning within the succession of tradition begun by the Apostles. Because the Reformers were already outside of that tradition by means of their theological inheritance from Rome, it was no surprise that they would depart further from it as they departed from Rome.

Without *sola scriptura*, all of Protestantism's distinctive doctrines are called into question. With it, however, one can go in nearly any theological direction and claim to be basing it in the Bible. For the Orthodox, however, the Church is the pillar and ground of the truth (1 Tim. 3:15).

One has to wonder how Western Christian history might have turned out differently if those second-generation Lutherans had read the letters of the Ecumenical Patriarch and used them to correct their own theology. Their respect for the purity of the East, however, was not greater than their devotion to their own theology, derived from their presuppositions in combination with an isolation from Orthodox tradition.

Unfortunately, this desire on the part of some Lutherans to connect with Orthodoxy quickly disappeared, and the various denominations of Protestantism continued their evolution. Today, most Methodists would not be recognizable to John and Charles Wesley, nor would most Lutherans be recognizable to Martin Luther, nor most Calvinists to John Calvin.

All that being said, the great love of traditional Protestants for the Scripture, and in many cases their devotion to history and tradition (albeit a much younger tradition), are points of contact between the churches of the Magisterial Reformation and the Orthodox Church. That contact has led many who formerly found their home in those churches to find a home in Orthodoxy, even in the twentieth century. These converts include at least one who became a martyr for the Orthodox faith, St. Elizabeth the New Martyr (1918), and the greatest writer of our time in the field of church history in English, Professor Jaroslav Pelikan of Yale University. There are also many former Lutherans, Calvinists, Anglicans, and Methodists among the Orthodox clergy.

There remains much work to do in terms of contact between these various traditions and the Orthodox tradition. Today, most are unaware that Orthodoxy even exists, and many Orthodox who might know Christians from those traditions have little to no knowledge of what they believe.

Four

The Radical Reformation

THE END OF ECCLESIOLOGY

It was the year 1817, and King Frederick William III of Prussia was upset. He was a member of the Reformed Church, and his wife Louise was a Lutheran. It was not their disparate church memberships that upset him, but rather the fact that he and the queen consort could not receive communion in each other's churches. King Frederick's solution to this problem was to order that the Reformed and Lutheran churches in Prussia unite into a single denomination in a legal act known as the Union of Prussia. The new, united denomination, called the Evangelical Christian Church, was founded on the notion of doctrinal pluralism (members did not have to adhere to the classic confessions of either Lutheranism or the Reformed churches) yet with a common liturgical and parish life.

What laid the groundwork for the Union of Prussia was a movement begun in the sixteenth century, initiated only shortly after the Magisterial Reformation. This movement had a number of influences, such as Pietism among Lutherans. What characterizes it most, however, is that it was not so much focused on denominations or church bodies as organizations; rather, it was a movement within various groups of theologians. This movement, which historians term the Radical Reformation, was a reaction not only against the perceived corruption and apostasy of the Roman Catholic Church, but also against the first Reformers, such as Luther and Calvin, who enjoyed state support for their churches.

The Radical Reformers felt that Luther and Calvin had not gone far enough in their reform, so they took the basic doctrinal presuppositions of the Reformation and carried their logic further. In this revolution within the revolution, the Radicals changed how Scripture was to be read, how church membership was understood, the meaning and practice of baptism, and in some cases, even the traditional doctrines about the identity of God. In many ways, the Radical Reformers simply took the doctrines of the first Reformers to their logical conclusions. Perhaps the most significant current within the Radical Reformation, however, was the growing notion that Christianity was a sort of private contract between the believer and God, which did not depend on membership in any church or any confession of doctrine.

The Radical Reform did eventually produce various denominations, but because its theology crossed denominational lines, in this chapter we will mainly focus our discussions on the movements and their doctrines.

MINDSETS AND MOVEMENTS

Pietism and Antinomianism

In the late seventeenth and eighteenth centuries, a movement sprang up primarily within German Protestantism known as Pietism. Pietism, a reaction against a perception of the mainstream Reformers as focusing too much on doctrine and institutions, sought to refocus the life of the individual believer on personal piety and commitment. What was important was not adherence to the beliefs of one or more of the Reformed confessions of faith, or membership in a particular church body—rather, individual experience came to be the defining characteristic of Christian life.

Pietism originally did not involve any break from the mainstream denominations forming in the seventeenth century—most Pietists were Lutherans. What it did, however, was to form little "churches within churches," small gatherings of believers for private devotions, Bible study, and so forth. This activity served to disconnect believers from a strong commitment to their local church as the formal community.

While the basic motivation for Pietism is something Orthodoxy can agree with—that is, a personal commitment to the life in Christ—the practices and results of the Pietistic movement are not something the Orthodox Church can laud. Pietism ultimately led to a general feeling that doctrine didn't matter very much and that the concrete life of the church as a community is of only secondary importance. But for the Orthodox, personal piety is the expression of the truths of Christian doctrine, and that piety only makes sense within the community.

One of the outgrowths of the Pietist movement's emphasis on individualism, particularly in its more radical sectors, came from a focus on the Reformation doctrine of *sola fide* (justification by "faith alone"). This theological phenomenon is called *antinomianism*, a term from Greek which means "against law." Antinomianism is a logical deduction from the doctrine of justification by faith alone. In antinomian thinking, if the believer is justified before God by his faith alone, then whether or not he lives a moral life is not critical and therefore optional.

Paired with the doctrine of eternal security—the teaching that it is impossible to lose salvation once you have it—antinomianism leads the Christian to believe that, because he's "been saved," he will go to heaven after death, even if he leads a life of selfishness and evil after his conversion to Christ.

Pietism in its more conservative form directly influenced the formation of the Methodist movement within the Anglican church. In its more radical forms, Pietism may be regarded as one of the most significant influences on all of modern-day Protestantism, especially evangelicalism with its emphasis on a "personal relationship with Jesus Christ" and its believers' tendency to change denominational or congregational allegiances several times in life. The individualism of Pietism is also one of the great currents that has affected the whole culture of the United States, which was founded in large part by English and German immigrants deeply influenced by Pietistic Christianity.

Scripture and Tradition

While the first Reformers believed in the doctrine of *sola scriptura* ("by Scripture alone"), their interpretations of the Scripture tended to remain in many respects very similar to the traditional interpretations of their Roman Catholic forebears. Even though they did not officially acknowledge the place of tradition in interpreting the Scripture, men like Luther were so influenced by tradition that they continued to make use of it in their theology. The Radical Reformers, however, especially those in the second generation of Protestantism, took *sola scriptura* to its logical extremes.

Tradition of any kind was rejected. The Radicals taught that Scripture was not merely the highest authority for Christians but the exclusive authority. Anything that appeared to contradict the Scriptures had to be "purified" from the church. For many of the Radicals, if the Scripture was silent on a subject, this meant that its practice was not merely optional but outright forbidden.

Yet this approach to the Bible raised the question of how one was to read the Scripture. For instance, most Christians throughout time who had read the Bible concluded that it taught that the bread and wine in the Eucharist were really changed to become the Body and Blood of Christ. But the Radicals taught that one should not believe that. Thus, while the Radical Reformation claimed to be rejecting tradition entirely, what it was actually doing was simply rejecting old tradition and replacing it with a new one. Without any continuous, authoritative tradition to inform and shape biblical interpretation, anyone may claim to be "just teaching the Bible." But why do people who make this claim all disagree with each other?

Many Baptist churches today profess the doctrine of soul competency. In this doctrine, each individual soul is ultimately responsible before God for its salvation. While the Orthodox can agree with this teaching in its essence, Baptists and others also hold it to mean that each believer has the full authority to interpret the Scripture for himself without correction from some other authority. The soul competency doctrine makes "every man his own pope" official doctrine.

The Radicals' approach to Scripture also led to congregationalism, which is the teaching that each local congregation is completely autonomous and may not be corrected by any authority outside itself. In some cases, this makes the local pastor a sort of pope in his own right, but in most congregations, it means that democratic rule controls not only the "business" side of the church, but even questions of doctrine and the hiring and firing of clergy.

In Orthodoxy, by contrast, the bishop stands in succession from the Apostles and exercises authority given by Christ, making him the center of local church unity and sacramental life. This tradition from the Apostles not only gives the bishop administrative authority but most especially, it makes him the president at the celebration of the Eucharist, which is the center of the Church's whole life. As St. Ignatius of Antioch, a disciple of the Apostle John who died in the second century, put it: "Wherever the bishop appears, the whole congregation is to be present, just as wherever Jesus Christ is, there is the whole Church" (*Epistle to the Smyrnaeans*, 8:2).

The whole church gathered around the bishop is the proper context of scriptural interpretation, and this holy gathering is the locus of Holy Tradition, the life in faith given by Christ to His Apostles and then passed down through the generations.

Anti-Clericalism and Anti-Sacramentalism

With the anti-traditionalism and congregationalism the Radicals promoted in their reading of Scripture, it was not long before a wholesale rejection of ordained ministry itself came into play. After all, if the Roman Catholic hierarchy with all its layers of clergy was corrupt, and if the Lutherans and Calvinists were corrupt for associating with the state, then perhaps the problem was the clergy itself.

Anti-clericalist feeling was exacerbated by the Zwinglian symbolic doctrines of the sacraments. The first Reformers reduced the sacraments in number to only two, baptism and the Eucharist. Zwingli and those who followed him, especially the Radical Reformers, further reduced the sacramental life by teaching that those two sacraments were only symbols, outward signs that represented God's grace. Therefore, if these ceremonies were really just symbols, then why was it necessary for them to be administered by an ordained clergy in proper succession from the Apostles?

Most of the Radical Reformers continued to have clergy leading their churches, but they were understood mainly as preachers and administrators, not as priests who offered up the sacrifice to God on behalf of the people. They certainly were not in any sense to be understood as a necessary element for church life. If need be, any group of believers could form themselves into their own congregation and appoint a pastor. If the rituals of Christianity are nothing special, then the priest is also nothing special.

The Radicals who rejected a sacramental priesthood regarded those who believed in it as superstitious believers in magic conducted by a class of tribal witch doctors. For a number of centuries up to that time, Latin theology had regarded the words spoken by the priest, *hoc est corpus meum* ("this is my Body"), as being the key moment in the Mass, when the bread was changed into Christ's Body. For the Radicals, *hoc est corpus meum* came to be slurred into "hocus pocus," which is now a phrase we commonly use to refer to a phony illusion.

Beyond a rejection of sacrament, the Radicals also tended to look with disdain upon church art. What was being rejected underneath all of this rhetoric was finally the traditional emphasis on the physical side of being spiritual. The Reformers had such a strong emphasis on reason and language that a fierce iconoclasm broke out throughout Europe. Churches were desecrated, statues torn down, and anything regarded as ostentatious or overly physical was denounced as idolatry. Such was the anti-materialism of the Radicals that their preferred church service came to be described with the motto, "four bare walls and a sermon."

For the Orthodox, this whole approach is deeply misguided. Man himself is composed of both body and soul, not just mind, and so his salvation involves the material world. The Son of God became incarnate as a real, concrete human being, and so it makes sense that we should physically eat His Body and drink His Blood, that icons can be made depicting Him and His saints, that churches should be made beautiful to glorify God, and that church services should be adorned richly to connect us with the splendor of heaven itself. A rejection of the material world in the Christian life is essentially an embrace of pagan dualism or of the fifth-century heresy of Nestorius, who taught that the "spiritual" Son of God and the "physical" Jesus Christ were two separate persons.

MAJOR DOCTRINES
Believers' Baptism

Before the Radical Reformation, most Christians still baptized infants in order to bring them into the Christian community. Although theology varied as to what baptism actually accomplished, there was still a general agreement that it accomplished something, even if that something was merely church membership and not a contribution to personal salvation. But the Radicals saw baptism as purely symbolic, merely an outward sign of God's spiritual work.

As the Radicals turned their anti-sacramental eye upon the Scripture, they could see baptism in several places in the New Testament. They could see that baptism always seemed to follow a profession of faith. They could also see that there is no explicit mention of infants being baptized. Thus, they reasoned that baptism should only be for those who make a clear profession of faith in Christ. And since they did not believe in any sacramental reality for baptism, they regarded it purely as an act of obedience on the part of the believer, not as an act of grace on the part of God. This is called *believers' baptism.*

In our own day, many who practice believers' baptism do not even regard it as a work of God, but rather merely as an obedience to His command to be baptized. In baptism, it is the believer who is making a statement about himself, not God making a change in the believer. At nearly every baptism I've attended where this doctrine is believed, the sermon from the pastor performing it always made the point that baptism doesn't actually do anything at all.

Some of the Radical Reformers even rejected the infant baptism believers had received while members of other churches, and they expected that such believers would be baptized again after making a profession of faith. Thus, some gained the name *Anabaptists,* which means "those who baptize again."

While it is true that there is no explicit passage in the New Testament in which infants are baptized (though it is hinted at in Acts 10 and 16 and 1 Cor. 1:16, where whole households were baptized, probably including small children), there is also no prohibition in the New Testament against it. Further, St. Paul connects New Testament baptism with Old Testament circumcision (Col. 2:11–12), which was administered to infants. Finally, though, the evidence for infant baptism lies in its practice throughout the whole history of the Church after the apostolic period.

Why would Christians, who give food, clothing, and shelter to their children, deny them the essentials of spiritual growth? We don't expect rational agreement when we feed them, so why should we expect rational agreement for them to be incorporated into Christ and His Church? After all, baptism contributes to our salvation (Mark 16:16; 1 Peter 3:21). In baptism, we put on Christ (Gal. 3:27), who commanded that children should be allowed to come to Him (Matt. 19:14; Mark 10:14; Luke 18:16).

Radical Reformation theology is essentially a rejection of history, however, and so the Radicals rejected arguments from the history of the Church that lacked explicit, undeniable reference in Scripture. There are internal problems with this teaching, however. Baptism cannot be administered to those who do not make a rational profession of faith, which means that it is not only denied to infants, but must logically be denied to those with severe mental retardation or mental illness—such a person could go his whole life and never be baptized.

Yet within the churches that practice believers' baptism, the very act of being baptized is usually considered optional. It has nothing to do with salvation and is simply an act of obedience on the part of the believer, making a public statement about his own faith. We do it because God commands it, but He gives no reasons for His commandment.

The Great Apostasy

As the Radical Reformers looked around and saw those who claimed to be Christians but who by their definition were most certainly not, it was only natural that they started to wonder what had become of the pure, primitive Church of the Apostles. How was it that true Christianity was absent for so long and that it had only recently been rediscovered during the Reformation?

Perhaps one of the most influential elements to come out of the Radical Reformation is the concept of the Great Apostasy. Those who believe in this teaching profess that at some point after the Apostles—whether immediately upon their death or later, such as at the time of Emperor St. Constantine the Great in the fourth century—the Church fell completely away and ceased to exist.

Calvinists teach something like the Great Apostasy doctrine, but it is modified in that the Church itself, not just individual believers, must always be reforming (*ecclesia semper reformanda*) and repenting of error. Thus, the Magisterial Reformers saw themselves not as rediscovering the Church but as helping to repair it and bring it back to primitive Christianity. But the Radicals saw things in a much more extreme light. Sebastian Franck, a sixteenth-century Bavarian among the Radicals, put it in stark terms:

> I believe that the outward church of Christ, including all its gifts and sacraments, because of the breaking in and laying waste of Antichrist right after the death of the apostles, went up into heaven and lies concealed in the Spirit and in truth. I am thus quite certain that for fourteen hundred years now there has existed no gathered church nor any sacrament. (*Epistle*, ca. 1530s)

This view is essential for those who follow the teachings of the Reformation, whether in its Magisterial or Radical forms, if they examine Christian history closely. After all, whether you pick the death of the Apostles or the time of Constantine as the end point of original, pure Christianity, it is clear that the vast majority of Christian history includes bishops, a belief in the true presence of Christ in the Eucharist, infant baptism, and so on. These many centuries of Christian history have to be explained somehow. The doctrine of the Great Apostasy is an attempt to explain it.

From the Orthodox point of view, there are many problems with this teaching. For one thing, it is a clear denial of Christ's promise in Matthew 16:18 that the gates of hell would not prevail against His Church. It is also an implicit denial of His headship of the Church, because how can the whole Church apostatize if He is a member? It also denies the place of the Church as the "pillar and ground of the truth" (1 Tim. 3:15). This teaching also raises this question: If the Church has been lost for all these years, how can you be sure that you are the one who has truly found it again?

One variant of the Great Apostasy doctrine taught by a minority of Baptists is called the Trail of Blood theory, which is also called Landmarkism (from Prov. 22:28, "Do not remove the ancient landmark which your fathers have set"). In this theory, it is taught that the institutional Church all fell away, but a remnant of true believers continued throughout the centuries, persecuted by the official Church (thus, *Trail of Blood*, the title of a book by J. M. Carroll).

"True" Baptists are traced through the centuries by identifying with various heretical groups, such as the Donatists, Novationists, and Montanists, all of whom have little in common with each other except that they opposed the mainstream Church, which Landmarkists identify as the Roman Catholic Church (ignorant of even the existence of Orthodoxy). With this theory, Landmarkists claim an unbroken historical connection to the Apostles, but the path by which it's claimed is truly bizarre. One would also have to wonder what Landmarkist Baptists would think if they were transported back in time to meet their imagined Baptist forebears, such as the Donatists, who argued for the real presence of Christ in the Eucharist; or the Novationists, who had set up their own bishop in Rome; or the Montanists, who claimed that their leader Montanus was the promised Comforter from Christ.

In any event, most of the Radical Reformers, and indeed, now most

Protestants of any stripe accept some form of the Great Apostasy doctrine, even if only implicitly. The true Church must have disappeared entirely at some point, or else there would be no point in reinventing it or rediscovering it. Those who accept this doctrine must also accept the implication that the Apostles fundamentally failed in their mission. Although the Apostles practiced pure Christianity, they failed to pass it on to their disciples.

The Orthodox Church teaches, however, that the apostolic mission did not fail. One need only look at the writings of someone like St. Ignatius of Antioch, who was a disciple of the Apostle John, to see that it was Orthodox Christianity, not Radical Reformation Protestantism, that was practiced by those who learned at the feet of the Apostles. Indeed, throughout the first few centuries of the Church's history, even before the time of Constantine, one of the marks of a church being trustworthy was that it could trace itself historically back to the Apostles. Apostolic succession was always defined by two elements: the continuity of both history (the succession of the laying on of hands) and maintenance of the same apostolic faith. Orthodoxy has kept both all the way until the present time.

Finally, one has to ask this question: If, as the Radical Reformers taught, we should not trust apostolic succession as a safeguard against heresy, then why should we trust someone whose authority extends only as far as his private reading room? How is one to judge between many different teachers who all claim to be led by the Holy Spirit?

The Invisible Church

Having rejected any sense of historical continuity through the centuries stretching back to the Apostles, and also having rejected the institutions of the Roman Catholic Church, the Lutherans, and other state-backed Reformed churches, it was only logical that the Radicals should ask themselves whether the outward organization of the Christian community had any theological value at all. That is, does the "visible" Church have any status in God's eyes?

With the Pietistic emphasis on individualism, the Radicals' answer to this question was "no." While the outward organization of churches might be useful in terms of helping believers live with one another, eternal salvation depended only on one thing: the believer's private relationship with God. And since the

Radicals had rejected sacraments and the priesthood, there was nothing any-one could offer the believer that he could not get for himself directly. Thus, for the Radicals, the "invisible" Church, composed of all true believers, wherever they may be found, was the only one that mattered. This teaching was further bolstered by the Radicals' de-emphasis on adherence to correct doctrine—one could be a "true Christian" whether one was Lutheran, Reformed, Zwinglian, or whatever else. (One is probably in significant doubt as a Roman Catholic, however.)

The Radicals were understandably reacting against a strong Western Christian emphasis on institution and organization, especially since their expe-rience of such things was tainted by the corruption that almost inevitably comes with official state sponsorship. When a church wields not only the Word but also the sword, much is risked.

In ancient times, some theological writers had drawn a distinction between the "visible" and "invisible" Church. The visible Church was recognizable in terms of concrete communities. It was a normal, traditional part of Christian life. But because there was never any guarantee that formal membership in the visible Church would grant one salvation, the idea was put forward of the "invis-ible" Church, whose true membership was known only to God. The tension between these two concepts was particularly explored by St. Augustine, who, as we have mentioned before, is a saint in the Orthodox Church, but whose writ-ings contain some theological error.

Orthodoxy makes no sharp distinction between the visible and invisible Church, however. While we agree that only God knows who will enjoy eternal salvation, whether they are formally Orthodox in this life or not, we also know that the final answer to that question must be deferred to the end of time. It is only in the eschaton, the age to come, that the fullness of the membership of the Church will be revealed. Until that time, the Church's mission is not yet complete. Further, Orthodoxy does not regard the visible Church as an orga-nization or institution, although it has those aspects. Rather, the Church is an organism, which has both exterior, visible elements and interior, invisible ele-ments, all governed by the Head, who is Christ. We must remember that Christ did not found a philosophical or ideological movement called "Christianity," but rather a concrete, historical community called the Church.

Repudiation of Core Dogma

Perhaps one of the most shocking elements of the anti-traditionalism of the Radicals came in the form of changes in some of the core doctrines of Christian belief. As some of the Radicals attempted to read the Bible divorced from prior tradition, they began to revive some of the ancient heresies. Known as Unitarians, certain of the Radical theologians even in the time of Luther rejected the doctrine of the Trinity and reasserted (as the heretic Sabellius did in the ancient Church) that Father, Son, and Holy Spirit were simply names, modes, or masks for a single divine Person. One such theologian (Michael Servetus) referred to traditional Trinitarianism as "that monstrosity of three realities," that "imaginary Trinity, three beings in one nature," which was actually tritheism.

This return to the heresies of the early centuries of the Church was denounced by the Magisterial Reformers such as Luther and Calvin, but their defense of the traditional creeds ultimately fell flat in the face of the common doctrine they all shared, *sola scriptura*. Since all the Reformers, whether the more traditional or the radical, shared a rejection of Church tradition, and since all shared an allegiance to *sola scriptura*, there was no authoritative way to answer the charge that one theologian's reading of the Bible was incorrect while another's was consistent with God's revelation.

While the Lutherans and Calvinists criticized these writers, claiming that they were departing from the Scripture by rejecting the traditional confessions, the Unitarians claimed to be defending "the older traditions of the Apostles." They claimed that if the classic dogmas were truly consistent with the Scripture, it "would certain have taught them somewhere in a manner that is clear, obvious, and free of verbal complications and ambiguities" (Faustus Socinus).

Many of the Unitarians and other revolutionaries in dogma believed that they were the first to see the true meaning of Scripture. One of the Unitarians, in referring to the Prologue of the first chapter of the Gospel of John, which speaks about the nature of God, claimed that it "has, as far as I know, never until now been correctly expounded by anyone" (Socinus). This writer went on to read this passage as clearly stating that Jesus Christ is not God and therefore not worthy of worship.

Those among the Radicals who repudiated traditional Trinitarian doctrine also rejected the various historic creeds of Christian history, most especially the Nicene Creed, which was regarded as a product of the "fall of the church" and engineered by Satan. St. Athanasius of Alexandria, whose profound writings on the Incarnation deeply influenced the First Ecumenical Council at Nicea, was called by one writer "the Antichrist." Another Radical Reformation theologian set forth a Christology that said the Son of God became man not "of the womb" of Mary, but rather simply "in the womb" (Menno Simons), which means that Jesus' humanity is a new creation, not an assumption of the humanity created in Adam. Mary becomes a kind of surrogate mother, and Jesus is not truly a member of our race.

Taking note of all this, it must be remembered that the majority of the Radical Reformers did not reject the traditional doctrines of Triadology and Christology that came out of the early centuries of the Church. Nevertheless, if *sola scriptura* means that all tradition and hierarchical authority are to be rejected and the Bible is to be read in an isolated manner, there can be no method by which theology is corrected and doctrinal orthodoxy maintained.

The assumption of these theologians that all Christian doctrine must necessarily be explicitly and systematically put forth in the Scripture is not one that the Orthodox share. Such a view fails to account for the nature of the Scriptural texts themselves. Nowhere does the Bible or even any passage in the Bible claim to be an all-sufficient handbook of Christian faith and life. Rather, it is a collection of writings whose purpose varies by occasion. Some are historical books, some poetry, some pastoral letters, some revelation, and some an account of personal experience with Jesus. Without the proper context to read the Church's book—namely, the Church—there is no way to be sure that one's interpretations are going to be correct.

DENOMINATIONAL FAMILIES

Anabaptists

The Anabaptists were so named because of their practice of insisting on believers' baptism, even for those who had been baptized before as infants. *Anabaptism* means "to be baptized again." Scholars disagree about the precise origin of the Anabaptist movements, but they mainly appeared in the sixteenth century in northern Europe, especially Germany and the Netherlands, as well as in what is now the Czech Republic.

The **Mennonites**, named for their founder Menno Simons (a former

Roman Catholic priest who joined the Anabaptist movement after the death of his pacifist Anabaptist brother), exist in multiple denominations in North America. Among the major denominations of the Radical Reformation, the Mennonites are largely regarded as the most conservative and most closely following the theology of the original Anabaptists. Among other distinctives, Mennonites tend to be pacifists.

One of the branches of the Mennonites is the **Amish,** who exist in several small denominations in the United States. Named for their founder Jacob Amman, the Amish were originally part of a movement to reform the Mennonite church. The Amish wanted the Mennonites to include the practice of shunning, social avoidance of those who had been baptized into the church but subsequently left. They also wanted to hold communion more often. Eventually, the Amish tended to withdraw themselves almost entirely from the world at large, based on the biblical call to be separate from "the world."

The Amish insist on simple living as part of the spiritual life, which usually includes a rejection of most modern technology. Their commitment to this principle is such that there are often dissensions over apparently trivial issues, such as how many buttons on one's shirt constitute vanity. The Amish now exist almost entirely in the United States and Canada, and while most speak English, they also speak a dialect of Old German that is often called Pennsylvania Dutch.

A group similar to the Amish who do not practice the same sort of deliberate separatism are the **Hutterites.** Hutterites are also committed to simple living but, unlike the Amish, they will often wear vibrant colors. Although they are unlikely to own televisions or most entertainment devices, they do not reject most modern technology as the Amish do. Like the Amish, the Hutterites speak their own dialect of German among themselves and live in communal colonies.

The **Brethren** are represented by numerous denominations both in the United States and abroad. Their theology is conservatively Anabaptist, and they have a number of distinctive practices. When they baptize, they do so by triple immersion (which is what the Orthodox do, as well). They also will accompany the reception of communion by a love feast, a common meal, a practice in the ancient Church that was originally connected with the Eucharist. They practice a ritual footwashing before receiving communion. In most respects, the Brethren denominations are quite similar to mainstream conservative Protestants.

The **Moravians** as a distinct community actually predate even the Magisterial Reformation, having their genesis in the teachings of Jan Hus, a fourteenth-century Roman Catholic priest and reformer in Bohemia and Moravia who wanted the church to conduct services in the local language (Czech), give the laity communion in both kinds (both the Body and Blood—practice at the time was to give the laity the Body only), and eliminate the teachings on purgatory and indulgences. Hus himself was eventually burned at the stake for heresy, but within about fifty years after his death, his followers organized themselves into a group called the Unitas Fratrum ("United Brethren," also "Bohemian Brethren"), who operated at first within the Roman Catholic Church. After the onset of the Reformation in Germany, the Hussites began to interact with Reformation theology and came to be similar to most believers in the Anabaptist movement. The Moravians, quite notably for the Orthodox, did not use the *Filioque* in the Nicene Creed. They both influenced and were influenced by the groups that became the Brethren, and they had two major settlements in North America—Bethlehem, Pennsylvania, and Salem, North Carolina (also called "Wachovia").

Anglican Offshoots

The Anglican Communion gave birth to several dissenting groups—most of those who left the Church of England were known as Dissenters. Most notable among them were the Methodists discussed in the previous chapter, who were heavily influenced by Pietism. The Presbyterians (mostly Scottish Calvinists) are also classified as Dissenters, but like the Methodists, were theologically and structurally more closely connected with the Magisterial Reformation.

Aside from the Methodists, however, the largest group of dissenters from the English church were known as **Puritans.** The Puritans, who flourished in the sixteenth and seventeenth centuries, were strongly Calvinist in their theology and urged the English to purify all "popery" from church life. The Puritans, like the Methodists who came much later, were essentially Pietistic in their basic outlook. Their strong emphasis on personal morality being enforced by public condemnation led in America to the well-known witch trials in seventeenth-century Massachusetts, and is also memorably depicted in Nathaniel Hawthorne's novel, *The Scarlet Letter*, in which an adulteress is forced to wear a red letter "A" in public.

Puritanism was the religion of the Pilgrims who landed at Plymouth (though they were known as the **Separatists**), and it is also the essential cultural element in the modern American fascination with scandal. It is also notable that Puritanism included a powerful work ethic, founded on the Calvinistic understanding of the predestination of the elect. It was believed that the elect would be materially successful in this life, and so Puritans and other Calvinists always worked hard out of a desire to prove their election to themselves and others. (This sense of being part of the elect is also what led the Puritans to be so confident in their condemnations of those they believed were demonstrably among the damned.) This work ethic is examined by the German economist and sociologist Max Weber in his classic work, *The Protestant Ethic and the Spirit of Capitalism*, first published in 1905. In a very real sense, it was the Puritans' need for assurance of their eternal election which led to the building of America.

The Puritans themselves suffered schisms, and one of the more significant was the **Quakers,** officially called the Religious Society of Friends. Nicknamed "Quakers" because of the physical "quaking" they exhibited in moments of mysticism, the Quakers believe that each Christian can and should experience God directly. Their mysticism tends to be practiced in group form rather than individually and typically occurs during meetings. Quaker meetings have no clergy, and members speak "as the Spirit moves them" within the meeting. Quakers believe that baptism is experienced as an inward reality, and so do not undergo a physical baptism ritual. Quakers also do not officially hold to *sola scriptura*, because they believe that the Holy Spirit would never lead them astray in their interpretation of the Bible. Over time, however, this belief led to divisions among Quakers when they disagreed over where God was leading them. Most modern Quakers, however, are not very concerned with theology as a normative set of doctrines and practices; instead, what they believe is most important is how God leads them in the moment. In this, they are clearly Pietistic in their outlook.

One group that broke off from the Quakers was the **Shakers,** who practiced a similar way of life and set of beliefs, though they tended to organize into separatist communes. The Shakers dwindled over time, however, as some members were attracted back into cities for work, and also because Shaker doctrine taught celibacy for all members. The Shakers began in the middle of the eighteenth century and attracted up to 200,000 converts over the next hundred years. As of 2006, there were only four still alive, living together in southern Maine.

Baptists

There are contradicting theories as to the origin of Baptists. They may be either an offshoot of the Anabaptist movement or possibly may have been founded by Puritans. (Anabaptists in England were known to have been called "Baptists" as early as 1569.) Whatever the case, the first Baptists as a distinct community appeared sometime in the late sixteenth or early seventeenth century.

Early Baptists were divided into two general camps, based on whether they accepted Calvinist or Arminian views on salvation. The Particular Baptists were generally Calvinistic, believing that God had a predestined elect set aside from before creation, while the General Baptists were Arminian, believing that the individual believer could choose to be saved. In our own time, Baptists may hold either view or may hold to a sort of hybrid view, in which the believer is responsible for choosing God initially, but then his free will is bound forever after that moment—he cannot again become "unsaved" once he is "saved." (This hybrid view is the most common.) Baptists who believe that salvation can be gained and then lost again are called Free Will Baptists. For most Baptists, however, salvation is a one-time event based on making a personal "decision for Christ," which, if made sincerely, makes a person "saved."

Most Baptists hold firmly to *sola scriptura*, but because every congregation has the right to decide its own doctrine, they do not all agree on what the Bible means. Nevertheless, because they share a common tradition, Baptists tend to share a common set of distinctive doctrines. They strongly believe in the individual believer's responsibility before God without any reference to the church community (this is called *soul competency* or *soul liberty*). They reject sacramental theology, regarding baptism and "the Lord's Supper" as "ordinances" commanded by Christ but not contributing in any sense to salvation. They also believe that the local congregation is the highest authority in church government. If a congregation does belong to a denomination, it is usually understood simply as an association or affiliation. The denomination holds no direct power over a local congregation. Ordination is usually for men only, but confers no special role. It merely acts as a sort of accreditation of a man's ability to lead and most especially to preach.

The Southern Baptist Conference is the single largest Protestant group in the United States, with about 16 million members and 42,000 churches. There are several other major denominations of Baptists in the United States, such as the General Association of Regular Baptists.

COMMON GROUND

The Radical Reformation in most respects was simply an expansion on the theological presuppositions of the Magisterial Reformation. With the doctrine of *sola scriptura* firmly in place, and informed by the anti-authoritarian streak that characterized the Radicals, the division into numerous factions and movements, all with different theology and practices, proceeded rapidly. More than anything else, the acceptance of the doctrine of the Great Apostasy led to an almost perpetual insistence from each new group that it had at last discovered or restored the true New Testament Church.

Like the Reformers before them, the Radicals did not understand themselves as innovating in doctrine or in practice. Rather, they believed they were returning Christians to ancient, pure, primitive Christianity. But without either tradition or hierarchy to guide them, their movements quickly split into a multitude of divisions, all claiming to have the corner on truth but without any historical or traditional evidence to authenticate their claims. Most especially because of the rejection of apostolic succession, the Radicals could give their followers no assurance that their doctrines were true. All common ground was based almost solely on mental agreement over how the Bible was to be read. Almost every time there was a disagreement led by a charismatic theologian, a new denomination was formed.

At its heart, the Radical Reformation is a rejection of the Incarnation. Most of the Radicals would of course adhere conceptually to the traditional dogmas about the Son of God becoming a man, but their theology and practice fail to reflect all the implications of the Incarnation. For the Orthodox, because God became a physical, material man, the Church has a concrete, historical reality. Ordination requires a physical act of laying on of hands. The Eucharist has a physical component to its spiritual reality. The physical act of baptism really accomplishes something spiritual. Icons are a witness to the Incarnation and an integral part of church life. All of these material elements in the ongoing salvation life of the Christian are rejected by the Radicals, and so we can only conclude that their theology of the Incarnation is lacking something at its heart. What was rejected in the Radical Reformation was the physical side of being spiritual.

There is much that the Orthodox have in common with various sectors of the Radical Reformation, most especially the insistence that the individual believer is accountable to God for his own salvation. But Orthodoxy sees and practices that accountability within the community of the Church, not as a separate contract the Christian has with God independently of any community. Further, Orthodoxy shares the Pietists' emphasis on living a life of devotion to God and His moral teachings. But at the same time, we believe that such a life is only possible if formed by the saving dogmas God has revealed to the Church through the Apostles.

I believe there is much hope today, however. Many of those who are coming to the Orthodox faith are coming precisely from the churches whose inheritance is from the Radical Reformation. I believe faith can be maintained as mainly a mental and emotional activity for only so long. We all must eventually reach out to the God who can truly be touched.

Five

Revivalism

THE NEW GNOSTICS

If the child given birth by the Radical Reformation was the idea that one could be a true Christian without church membership, then Revivalism is what that idea looks like fully grown. While the sixteenth- and seventeenth-century Radicals reacted against the dry confessionalism of the magisterial churches with an emphasis on personal piety, their heirs in the Revivalist movements turned that Pietism into a truly popular movement that could be embraced by the masses, retaining nearly all of the doctrinal positions of the Radicals.

We saw in the previous chapter how the Radicals distanced themselves from all the material elements of traditional Christianity. They retained no priesthood, no sacraments, no holy places, no asceticism, no place for visual beauty in worship. Yet they did retain a sense of *community*, if not really *church* as it had been understood for centuries. With all of those traditional defining elements of the sacred Christian community removed by the Radicals, Revivalism took the next logical step and dispensed with the necessity for community altogether. Instead of a church, a concrete, historical community governed by structure and dogma, Revivalism was a *movement*, a popular uprising defined by enthusiasm, emotion, and personal charisma.

We are defining Revivalism here in fairly broad terms to refer to the characteristic Christian life and worship that finds its origins in the eighteenth- and nineteenth-century "Great Awakenings," mainly occurring in the United States. Revivalism has had different levels of influence on American Christianity, but there is virtually no Christian in America who has not been touched by the culture Revivalism created. With the advent of Revivalist religious culture, American Christianity as it is known to this day was born. This movement is often called Evangelicalism, but that term itself is hard to define these days, especially since it has been taken up by the popular media. It would not be an exaggeration to say that the vast majority of Protestants in the United States are Revivalists to some extent.

We saw earlier how the ancient gnostics were the first heretics in the Church. Gnosticism was sharply marked by individualism, the belief that salvation was ultimately a private matter rather than a communal experience. The gnostics also stressed that salvation was obtained by saving knowledge rather than by faithful participation in sacramental church life. The gnostic religious system was strongly dualistic, believing that "spiritual" things were good, while the physical world was evil or at best unimportant. In its understanding of salvation and of culture in general, gnosticism was also profoundly escapist, seeking to withdraw from the world. Gnosticism placed a heavy emphasis on personal ecstatic experience contrasted with the "ordinary" ritual and sacramental life of most Christian believers.

In this chapter, it is our assertion that much of modern Protestantism, because of the influence of Revivalism, has essentially become gnostic. As we describe various attitudes, doctrines, and behaviors, it is necessary to understand that any given believer influenced by the Revivalist movement may subscribe to only a selection of the many elements that together make up the characteristics of the movement.

Revivalism as a movement has a number of historical moments that might be described as a point of origin. In the 1730s and 1740s, the First Great Awakening swept through the British colonies in America, reshaping the lives of existing believers and bringing Christianity to the slave population. The Second Great Awakening came at the end of the eighteenth century and the beginning of the nineteenth, marked by mass revival meetings and great missionary efforts as various denominations competed for dominance, especially in the expanding American West. These two movements are what truly brought the Methodist and Baptist denominations into their own. The final major movement that shaped Revivalism in America was begun in 1906 at the Azusa Street Revival, which was the spark that ignited the Charismatic Pentecostal movement.

Individualism

When I was in college, one of the courses I took covered the early centuries of Christianity, studying the writings of the Christians who followed immediately in the footsteps of the Apostles. After a few weeks of study, one student in the class raised his hand, apparently a bit frustrated. When the professor called on him, he said, "You know, I don't see anything in here about accepting Jesus into your heart as your personal Lord and Savior."

That moment underlined for me how ignorant the children of Revivalism are of the character of Christianity at the time of its origins. Of course there is nothing in the writings of the early Church Fathers about "accepting Jesus into your heart as your personal Lord and Savior," because such a formulation had nothing to do with becoming a Christian. But that formula so defines Christianity for many believers in our own time that they find the writings of the disciples of the Apostles and their immediate successors to be alien.

For some of the spirit of what drives this approach to Christian life, let's look at an example of how it's preached. On July 8, 1741, in the town of Enfield, Connecticut, Congregationalist preacher Jonathan Edwards stood up and preached a sermon that has now become a classic in the Revivalist movement. This sermon, the well-known "Sinners in the Hands of an Angry God," which probably took close to an hour to preach, includes such words as these:

> And let every one that is yet out of Christ, and hanging over the pit of hell, whether they be old men and women, or middle aged, or young people, or little children, now hearken to the loud calls of God's word and providence. This acceptable year of the Lord, a day of such great favour to some, will doubtless be a day of as remarkable vengeance to others. . . . God seems now to be hastily gathering in his elect in all parts of the land; and probably the greater part of adult persons that ever shall be saved, will be brought in now in a little time, and that it will be as it was on the great out-pouring of the Spirit upon the Jews in the apostles' days; the election will obtain, and the rest will be blinded. If this should be the case with you, you will eternally curse this day, and will curse the day that ever you was born, to see such a season of the pouring out of God's Spirit, and will wish that you had died and gone to hell before you had seen it. . . . Therefore, let every one that is out of Christ, now awake and fly from the wrath to come. The wrath

of Almighty God is now undoubtedly hanging over a great part of this
congregation. Let every one fly out of Sodom: "Haste and escape for your
lives, look not behind you, escape to the mountain, lest you be consumed."

The stereotype of the "fire and brimstone" preacher finds its origins in
Revivalism. The purpose of this kind of sermon is to make the listener strongly
aware of his personal guilt before God, bolstered quite often with graphic
depictions of the damned suffering in hell. Once the listener is in a sufficient
state of fear for his eternal life, he is then led by the preacher to make a "personal
commitment to Christ." He may be led in praying the "sinner's prayer," which
typically includes an acknowledgment of personal sin, a sincere statement of
repentance, a statement of belief in Christ's death and resurrection, followed by
a request for Jesus to "come into [his] heart" and grant him salvation from sin.
The sinner's prayer may also include an acknowledgment of Jesus as "Lord of
my life," but that is not usually considered absolutely essential. A key element is
that this prayer must be prayed with utmost sincerity.

You may have some experience of this tactic yourself if you have ever had
anyone approach you and ask, "If you were to die tonight, do you know beyond
all shadow of a doubt where you would spend eternity?" Those who willingly
submit to this whole process are then told that they are now Christians bound
for heaven, and usually (though not always) they are also told that they will go
to heaven no matter what they do from now on. They are now among a special
group called the "saved," and everyone who does not belong to it is "unsaved" or
"lost." Your salvation is ultimately between you and God, and the "church" consists of everyone who is "saved," whether they belong to a church community or
not. This may be called "making a decision for Christ." Such a strong emphasis
is laid on a one-time personal conversion as a critical element of salvation that
those raised as Christians from birth may sometimes be at a loss to find that
moment in their lives. Even those who do experience such a moment may wonder whether that moment was "real" or not. And logically, one has to wonder if
profoundly retarded people can get "saved."

A careful study of this phenomenon shows that what happens in these
experiences is radically different from traditional Christianity in general and
Orthodoxy in particular. Nowhere in any of this is there a reference to the
Church, the Body of Christ. Baptism is not in any way involved. There is no

sense that salvation itself critically involves anything other than escaping from hell after death. The only thing you are "saved" from is hell. The whole process is essentially private, mental, and emotional. There is no ongoing life of struggle against the sinful passions.

We may contrast this model of salvation with that of St. Paul, which did of course include a change of heart (Acts 9:3–9). But his conversion is also communal, in that God told him to go and listen to Ananias to learn what he must do (9:6). It is ascetical, as he fasts for three days (9:9). It is finally sacramental, for Ananias also baptizes him (Acts 9:18). Nowhere in this most iconic of New Testament conversions do we see salvation defined in such limited terms as in the sinner's prayer model.

The basic religious impulse behind the individualism of Revivalism is a good one, that the believer has to decide for himself to do what is right and good before God, to change his life. But where this attitude differs from Orthodoxy is that the Orthodox Church says that making a decision is only the beginning. Realizing you are a sinner is good, and repenting of your sins is good, but we will probably never be truly aware in a single moment of the depth of sin that most of us hide in our hearts. A life of continual repentance is called for, not because doing so earns one salvation, but because doing so is a cooperation with God so that He may bring salvation and personal transformation into every part of our humanity.

Further, perhaps the most sadly characteristic part of Revivalist individualism is that it is inherently anti-communal. Certainly, many believers of this sort do belong to church communities. But that belonging is usually in terms of "fellowship" or "help for the Christian life" rather than a participation in the Body of Christ regarded as critical to salvation. Further, because of the completely non-sacramental approach to Christianity of Revivalism, there is ultimately nothing available at church that is not also available at home or out in the woods.

It is not hard to see the origin of the now-common attitude of those who say they are "spiritual but not religious." Having been told there is nothing critical to their salvation available only in the church community, they find that being "spiritual" is much easier without all those pesky other believers to get in the way. Having been told or having learned through culture that personal salvation (or "enlightenment") is a private matter between them and God, they find they are much more comfortable obeying only their own interpretations of Scripture or "spiritual experience" rather than having a pastor or confessor. Tradition is absolutely in no way needed, because the private individual is the measure of everything.

Ralph Waldo Emerson, the nineteenth-century hero of individualists everywhere, once wrote, "A true man belongs to no other time or place, but is the centre of all things. Where he is, there is nature" (*Self-reliance*). The heresy of individualism is the rejection of communion, which is absent from the "sinner's prayer" approach to salvation, whether it is the communion of the People of God with each other or with God Himself in Jesus Christ. The twentieth-century Orthodox saint, Silouan the Athonite, said, "My brother is my life." For him, community life is critical to his own salvation. But the motto of the "sinner's prayer" type of salvation might instead be, "Am I my brother's keeper?"

In the Orthodox Church, there is a common saying: "We are saved together, but damned alone." Salvation is not a private matter. It is a communion of persons, becoming one with God and with Christ's Body, the Church. Christ Himself defined eternal life not as the private "fire insurance" of getting out of hell, but rather as truly knowing the true God (John 17:3).

It is perhaps no coincidence that Emerson, once a minister in the Unitarian Church, eventually rejected all forms of Christianity altogether because of his hatred of the ritual of Holy Communion.

Gnosis: Faith as Knowledge and Eternal Security

We made reference earlier to that question of the Revivalist evangelist: "Do you know where you will spend eternity?" One of the marks of the Revivalist understanding of salvation is a desire for absolute certainty, knowing beyond all doubt that heaven will be one's eternal destination. This desire for epistemological certainty is called "faith," but it is not the understanding of faith the Orthodox see in the New Testament and throughout their whole tradition.

The early gnostics could not accept the "ordinary" trust and faith that characterized the average believer in the early Church, and so they sought out *gnosis*, "knowledge" of their salvation, an absolute inner assurance and certainty that they would be saved. The fundamental problem with this approach is that it is not faith! In Greek, "faith" is the word *pistis*, which like almost any word ending in *-is* refers to a progressive, ongoing, dynamic reality. A more accurate, though perhaps clumsier, translation might be "faithing." In the apostolic faith represented in the New Testament and for all twenty centuries of Orthodox Church life, faith is not understood as a single, absolute certainty, based on a one-time event of "salvation."

Those who define "faith" as an absolute knowledge are not following in the tradition of the Apostles, but rather in the tradition of the eighteenth-century "Enlightenment" in Europe and America, which elevated human reason and sought to give mankind perfect assurance of whatever it might try to know. While the Enlightenment led many to abandon religion because it is "irrational," many more applied the Enlightenment's principles to religion, redefining the experience of dynamic faith as a mental surety of knowledge. Absolute knowledge became defined as "faith," and the true meaning of faith was forgotten by many.

Those who preach the doctrine of faith as knowledge will often quote verses like 1 John 5:13 to back up their claims: "These things I have written to you who believe in the name of the Son of God, *that you may know that you have eternal life*, and that you may continue to believe in the name of the Son of God" (emphasis added). Yet the word in that verse for "know" is not the Greek term for rational, mental certainty, *epistemi*. Rather, it is *eidite*, which is a knowledge based on something one sees and experiences, not something one is mentally certain of.

Nowhere in the Scripture or in the consensus of the Fathers do we see the notion that faith is just an inner, mental knowledge or even a feeling. Faith is rather an ongoing, dynamic relationship of trust and cooperation of the believer with God. Faith is a life of communion. Just as a marriage is not made merely by the wedding ceremony or the exchange of rings, salvation is not made by making a single decision for Christ. It is merely begun by that act, and like marriage, which St. Paul uses as a metaphor for salvation in Ephesians 5, salvation must be maintained and nurtured in order to come to full fruition.

There are really two errors here: the mistaking of faith for knowledge, and the resultant error of what is called *eternal security*, popularly known as "once saved, always saved." Because the believer thinks he has absolute certainty of his salvation, he has been led to believe that no matter what he now does for the rest of his life, he is "saved." But even in the Scripture itself, there is much language that would make no sense if salvation were a single, past event that is absolutely certain. Nor is there any indication from Scripture that God will honor our free will for one moment to save us and then violate it for the rest of our lives to keep us from falling away. It should be enough, however, to quote the words of Christ in Matthew 10:22; 24:13; and Mark 13:3: "He who endures to the end will be saved."

Even in other problems in life, the understanding of faith as knowledge leads people to think that if only they can convince themselves of something they otherwise would believe not to be true, then miracles can be performed. If they have cancer, they can be cured only if they have enough "faith." But this isn't faith. It's just an exercise in self-delusion. Faith in such a circumstance is trusting God and drawing closer to Him no matter what He might choose to permit.

One of the unfortunate side-effects of the Revivalist transmutation of faith into knowledge is that some believers whose Christian life is defined by this sense of absolute certainty can begin to regard themselves as prophets. What in traditional Christian terms might be described in terms such as "I believe that perhaps I should . . . ,""Maybe God is leading us to . . . ," or "It could be that God is showing me . . ." may be put in these sorts of terms instead: "God is telling me to . . . ,""This is what the Lord wants me to do," or "God's plan for us is . . ." This kind of talk is common in Pentecostal circles, where it is often assumed that frequent supernatural interventions by God (such as speaking in tongues) are a mark that one is saved.

It is true that we can say with certainty what God has revealed to all of us, such as that He wants us all to be saved, that He wants all of us to repent of our sins, that He wants all of us to bring the Gospel to those around us. The danger comes when the believer starts to see himself as God's mouthpiece of specific and new revelation. Such people may say that God has given them "a word" for someone else, and they express themselves in highly direct and certain terms, believing they speak for God, not just in the prophetic ministry we all have to bring the world the Gospel, but also with detailed, direct instructions not only for themselves but also for others. In this, they not only claim to be a spiritual father or mother for another but also to be clairvoyant.

Although this behavior may be sincere and arise from a desire to serve God, it should be carefully checked, because it is spiritual delusion to presume a prophetic role, especially in regard to others. True clairvoyance is rare, even among the saints, and those gifted with it usually try to flee from it rather than enthusiastically bringing it to others. In any case, a spirituality divorced from the stabilizing community life of the Church, apart from the context of obedience to an experienced father-confessor, will always tend toward deviation.

Dualism

In the Revivalist religious system, just as with the gnostics, salvation has nothing to do with the material world. To be sure, most Christians influenced by Revivalism believe that morality has a material component—that what you do with your body, for instance, is important—but this moral outlook is uninformed by the traditional Christian understanding of the role of creation in salvation and man's place in creation. Therefore, Revivalist Christianity is strongly dualistic. Christians who preach that material reality has a role in salvation itself are usually regarded by Revivalists as superstitious or even idolatrous.

With this dualistic worldview, Revivalist Christianity has no sacraments to speak of. If a believer gets baptized or takes communion, such acts are understood as mere obedience, "ordinances," or symbols of a "spiritual" reality, signs of an absent presence. Baptism in no way saves. Communion in no way saves. Yet St. Peter says in 1 Peter 3:21 that baptism saves us. Christ says in Mark 16:16, "He who believes and is baptized will be saved." And the Lord also says in John 6:53, "Most assuredly, I say to you, unless you eat the flesh of the Son of Man and drink His blood, you have no life in you." But Revivalist doctrine reads all these passages with its dualistic bias, seeing them as pure symbol with no material component.

Like ancient gnosticism, the dualism of Revivalist Christianity inherently denies the Incarnation of Jesus Christ, that God became a man. The gnostics were explicit in their denials, and St. Ignatius of Antioch in the second century points out that you can always spot the gnostics in the congregation because they refuse to take Holy Communion (*Smyrnaeans* 7:1). After all, if God became a man and invites us to eat and drink His Body and Blood—an invitation that scandalized many of Jesus' disciples in John 6, such that some left Him—then the sacraments as a physical experience make perfect sense. This is why receiving Communion in an unworthy manner can be damning (1 Cor. 11:29). If the bread and wine do not truly become Christ's Body and Blood, then how could receiving mere symbols ever be so dangerous? Yet the Scripture says otherwise.

While most Revivalists would not deny the Incarnation, the fact that God became man, they deny all the traditional results of the Incarnation—the sacraments, the priesthood, the holy icons, and all the physical components of Christian life for twenty centuries. These things are all witnessed to in the history of the Church, that this way of life was normal for the Christians who sat at the Apostles' feet and then for their own disciples. It takes either a profound ignorance of history or a denial of its authority to turn away from the physical side of being spiritual. Thus, we have to regard this approach as an implicit denial of the Incarnation rather than an explicit one.

The dualism of Christian Revivalism extends far beyond the sacramental life. Without a sense of the essential physical element of spiritual life, Christian anthropology—the theology of what mankind is and how it can be saved—suffers. If your body doesn't really matter, there is no need for asceticism. (Eat, drink and be merry!) How could fasting, vigils, and chosen periods of sexual chastity have any effect on the spiritual life? All of these kinds of practices, which are evident in Holy Scripture, are rendered meaningless in the dualistic worldview, and one will find that while some lip service may be paid to them among Revivalists, they are generally completely absent. Or if they are present, they are regarded as extraordinary acts of piety rather than as a lifestyle that trains the body to be submissive to the soul and thus brings salvation even to the body.

The dualism of Revivalism also has an environmental impact. Traditional Christian anthropology teaches that man is not merely the steward of creation, but its priest. But with no sacraments, no altar, and no worldview that can see the physical as holy, creation is simply something to be exploited, something to be used. Environmentalists are right in criticizing this approach to our world, though they do so for the wrong reasons. While environmentalists often elevate "Mother Nature" over mankind, the Orthodox Christian sees mankind as a priest and creation as his church. How could a priest ever desecrate his own church? How could he not see it as God's gift to him, to be offered up on the altar, sanctified by grace, and then returned to him for his salvation?

This anti-materialism has further ramifications. For most Revivalists, history also makes no difference for the Christian life. Yet what is Christian history but the continuous extension of the Incarnation? The Church must have no concrete reality to it, either. There is no place or person or act one can point to and say, "Here is the Church." Rather, the Church exists only as an invisible reality, a collection of all true believers everywhere, who might disagree profoundly over doctrine and practice, over the very meaning and application of the Gospel, yet are still somehow all "the Church."

Dualism has an effect on morality, as well, especially those areas that involve the body. Many believers in our time, even serious Christians, have a hard time understanding just why it could be wrong to give oneself sexually to another without being joined in Christian marriage. If you've ever tried to teach this to a teenager, you know it's a hard sell, even on rational grounds. But Orthodox tradition teaches us that there is a spiritual union that occurs along with the physical union.

There is a spiritual reality to all the food we eat, which is why we ask God to bless it before eating it, don't eat too much of it, and then thank Him for it afterward. It's why eating together is one of the most profound expressions of human community. This moral theology of the body is not merely a matter of obedience to the divine command and fear of reprisal for disobedience—it stems from an understanding of the mystical reality of the creation itself. If God is in every atom and molecule of every thing, then holiness is everywhere, especially in those places and things that He has particularly blessed.

So what can we conclude regarding a spiritual outlook that denies history, liturgy, sacrament, icon, asceticism, concrete community, and a profound sense of the holiness of all creation? It can only be regarded as an implicit denial of Christ's Incarnation.

Yet the spiritual man, though he cannot live by bread alone, also cannot live without bread. He needs physical activity in his spiritual life. He needs a church building to go to. He needs songs to sing. He needs books to read and spiritual images to put in front of his eyes. Revivalism cannot suppress the basic spiritual need that mankind has for physical elements in the spiritual life. But because of the divorce from Christian history and tradition, because of the divorce from the historic Church, Revivalism has sought out a new bride. This bride is what we might call the "Spirit of the Age." This marriage of believers with a new spirit is why such believers have welcomed pop music and rock-n-roll into their churches. It is why there is a lucrative industry dedicated to creating a "Christian" niche market. It is why emotion is mistaken for spirituality. It is why sentiment is substituted for holiness. Instead of icons of Christ, whose piercing stare calls you to repentance, the Revivalist can go to a Christian bookstore and buy a soft-focus, long-haired picture of Jesus, which a friend of mine calls "the benevolent rock-n-roller."

All of this amounts to a kind of pseudo-Incarnational approach to the physical side of being spiritual, and it is honestly no wonder that when the world looks at this and is told that it is "Christianity," it easily turns away. After all, the world's rock-n-roll is, quite frankly, better rock-n-roll. (Having been a professional stagehand for ten years, I assure you that this is so!) Rather than transforming and transfiguring culture, as the Church has traditionally done, Revivalist Christianity has instead been transformed by culture. The winds of fashion, fad, and political correctness blow where they may, and Revivalism is too often content to float like a leaf on the wind. This behavior is what gives Revivalism its strong tendency to keep changing, to seek after the latest new means of attracting church attendance, always to be looking for some innovation. A church that is essentially Revivalist will almost certainly change its doctrines every time it changes pastors. Yet for the Orthodox, if you attend an Orthodox service anywhere in the world, you will hear the same faith preached, the same faith in the liturgy, the same faith lived by serious believers.

Escapism and the Rapture

As part of the dualistic worldview of Revivalist Christianity, such believers often have a strong escapist streak. Because this world is not something holy which needs to be rescued and re-offered to God, the believer ultimately desires to withdraw himself from it. This manifests itself in several ways. One of the most obvious is the attempt to create an Evangelical subculture with its own lingo, branding, and niche markets. Instead of Malibu Barbie, you can get "Christian" Barbie. Instead of watching "worldly" movies, you can watch "Christian" ones. And so forth.

This escapism also feeds into the general Revivalist approach to the physical world itself. Presbyterian pastor Philip J. Lee, in his book *Against the Protestant Gnostics* (p. 190), details an interesting account regarding American Secretary of the Interior James Watt. The *Wall Street Journal* asked the secretary in the early 1980s, when he had just taken steps to permit massive exploitation of planetary resources, often including strip mining, the sell-off of National Park land, and so forth, whether he was worried about future generations and their ability to live in and enjoy the land. Mr. Watt, no doubt a Christian of Revivalist tendencies, replied, "I do not know how many future generations we can count on before the Lord returns."

But what is perhaps the most striking element of the escapism in this belief system is a powerful fascination with the end of the world. This period of history is perhaps the only one that really interests Revivalists. I can recall from my own youth how a number of the Evangelical churches my family attended seemed to base the vast majority of sermons on the Book of Revelation.

There is something titillating about the idea of looking into the future, and even though the Bible explicitly warns against making any predictions of when the Second Coming of Christ will occur (Matt. 25:13), there have been various Revivalist leaders who have given exact dates when the end of the world would come, often included in the pages of bestselling books. Even without making specific predictions, Revivalist Christianity has a strong orientation toward eschatological expectation, believing that the eschaton, the end of the world, is nigh. Perhaps the most popular event in this expectation is what is commonly called the *Rapture*.

The most basic version of the Rapture doctrine goes something like this: When the end of the world is approaching, Jesus will appear in the sky, hover there, and all true believers will then be "raptured" up into the air to follow Jesus back to heaven. What happens after that is a matter for some debate, whether there are seven literal years of a "Great Tribulation" or whether that will have already been happening for a while or be ending at that moment. Armageddon may happen before or after, as well. There is also some debate over whether anyone will notice the Rapture is occurring. In any case, this Rapture takes place before the final Second Coming of Christ.

This belief is cobbled together from several biblical passages, but most especially from 1 Thessalonians 4:16–17: "For the Lord Himself will descend from heaven with a shout, with the voice of an archangel, and with the trumpet of God. And the dead in Christ will rise first. Then we who are alive *and* remain shall be caught up together with them in the clouds to meet the Lord in the air. And thus we shall always be with the Lord." But this passage nowhere talks about Jesus hovering. For the Orthodox, these verses are about the end of the world. When Christ comes back, the general resurrection will occur, and time as we know it will end. In a moment, it will all be over.

What many Rapturists do not know is that their particular form of belief is less than two hundred years old. Some historians trace this belief to the supposed visions of a Scottish teenager named Maggie MacDonald, whose influence was eventually felt by Cyrus Scofield, whose *Scofield Reference Bible* included Rapturist doctrine and was wildly popular among Revivalists in the nineteenth and twentieth centuries. Others point to different sources of origin. Whatever may be the case, it is generally agreed that it was not until about the nineteenth century that people started believing in the Rapture as it is now commonly taught. This doctrine is pervasive, and one may find people who believe in it across many denominations. It is so common that Rapturist believers who encounter those who disagree with them are often taken aback, as though their interlocutors were denying belief in the divinity of Jesus. But the majority of the world's Christians, including Roman Catholics, Orthodox Christians, traditional Anglicans, and many in the Reformed denominations, have never believed in Rapturist doctrine.

The Rapture is so popular that it is represented in novels and movies (such as the popular *Left Behind* series starring Kirk Cameron) and even video games. There's actually a website you can send money to that will send an email to all your "unsaved" friends after you get raptured, letting them know what's happened to you and that they should repent soon (YouveBeenLeftBehind.com). One popular Rapture bumper sticker says, "In case of Rapture, this car will be unmanned." And one somewhat less popular bumper sticker replies with, "In case of Rapture, can I have your car?"

Far from being simply a quaint and fanciful set of teachings about the end of the world, however, this variety of eschatology is spiritually dangerous. Those who believe in it are waiting for its occurrence and can rest assured that if it hasn't yet occurred, they still have time to live however they want. This especially holds true for those who believe that the Rapture will save them from the Antichrist. But what if an Antichrist comes, but the Rapture hasn't happened? Will such believers follow him, thinking he can't really be the one because they haven't been raptured?

Coupled with Rapturist belief is often the return of an ancient heresy called *chiliasm*, the belief that Christ's Second Coming will be followed by a literal thousand years of rule here on earth. Though this belief was held by some early Christian writers, it was eventually rejected by the Church as inconsistent with apostolic tradition, a rejection that was codified into the Nicene Creed with the phrase, "And He shall come again with glory to judge the living and the dead, *whose kingdom shall have no end*" (emphasis added).

Experience and Enthusiasm

The strong individualism of Revivalist Christianity, because it is detached from the traditional sacramental community life of the historic Church, came to long for something else to tie its communities together, some way for the individual believer to have some assurance of his salvation. The sense of belonging is traditionally strong for those who participate in liturgical Christianity, but for those whose worship includes no liturgy, there has to be something else to connect the believer to God and to his fellow Christians. For Revivalism, this something can be described in two terms, *experience* and *enthusiasm.*

With their emphasis on individual conversion, Revivalists love few things better than a good conversion story. The best ones are those told by "dirty" sinners who have reformed. Liars, cheats, and those who harbor hatred, gluttony, envy, and judgment in their hearts are less interesting than those with more "spectacular" sins such as murder, drug addiction, and sexual depravity. (The "home run" of conversion stories is reserved for those who used to belong to non-Christian religions, most especially supposed "Satanists.") The key in all these stories is a personal experience that can be passed on, especially one with strong emotional content. This passing on is usually referred to as "testifying." Hearing these things may inspire some listeners to want to have a similar experience. Believers are encouraged to develop their own personal salvation narratives, called "testimonies," to aid them in recruiting others for the faith. Preaching in Revivalist churches is often marked by this tendency toward enthusiastic emotionalism and insistence on a personal experience.

This desire for an enthusiastic experience can often become so intense that believers begin to lay great stress on seeing miraculous manifestations of the work of the Holy Spirit, usually accompanied by rousing, emotionally stirring music and frenetic preaching. Usually, what is experienced and witnessed is claimed to be the same as what the Apostles experienced on the Day of Pentecost in the New Testament, and so the term Pentecostal is frequently used. Because these are supposedly "gifts" from God, they may also be called **charismatics** (from the Greek *charismata*, "gifts"). Pentecostals claim to perform "faith healing," exorcisms, and, most characteristically, to be able to speak in private prayer languages known only to them and God, usually called "speaking in tongues." Some groups of Pentecostals will go so far as to claim that if a believer does not speak in tongues, he is not really "saved." The first time a person speaks in tongues may be called a "baptism of the Holy Spirit," which is considered separate from and more crucial than water baptism.

Such supposedly miraculous happenings are often manifested by people being overcome with emotion, perhaps knocked to the ground, jumping up and down, running in circles around the church, and even in some cases, barking, growling, and making other animal sounds. To those inexperienced in Pentecostal forms of religion, such people may appear to be having seizures or to be possessed.

The Orthodox have never put a strong condemnation on the practice of speaking in tongues, but at least one Orthodox saint, John Chrysostom, said that such things were no longer needed, because the Church had come fully into the world. Even then, many Orthodox do not regard modern Pentecostalism as exhibiting what happened on Pentecost itself, which was sober and focused on preaching the Gospel to other people in their own languages. The Scriptures say to "test" the spirits (1 John 4:1), but most of what happens in Pentecostal congregations is accepted as being from the Holy Spirit without any stable process of discernment. One twentieth-century Orthodox writer who studied the modern charismatic phenomenon in some detail in the early 1970s, Fr. Seraphim Rose, said there was certainly a supernatural spirit involved in the Pentecostal movement, but it was not the Holy Spirit (in *Orthodoxy and the Religion of the Future*).

This strong emphasis on the Holy Spirit, sometimes to the detriment of the Father and the Son, may be understood as a reaction against the dryness of much of Western theology, born out of the acceptance in the West of the *Filioque* clause added to the Creed by the Roman Catholic Church, which makes the Holy Spirit subordinate to the Father and the Son. It is a theological backlash against academic theology and rationalism.

Even if a particular Revivalist congregation does not practice these so-called "gifts of the Spirit," there is often still an **anti-intellectualist** streak in its religious culture. Especially in many rural congregations, if the preacher never went to any seminary or even to college, it is to his *credit*, because such things just confuse you and rob you of true faith. As we saw earlier, this is the natural fruit of Pietism with its insistence on personal spiritual experience rather than on adherence to doctrine. This anti-intellectualism fits in well with a denial of the importance of history for Christian life, as well as bolstering the doctrine of *sola scriptura*, where it's just "me and my Bible," without any interference from snobbish academics or authoritarian figures.

Besides Pentecostalism, the desire for personal experience coupled with individualism has birthed another strain in Revivalist religion, the shift toward making Christianity into a self-help program. This approach is particularly seen in many modern mega-churches, which try to appeal to "seekers," giving them whatever they might want to bring them through the door. This kind of religion, shaped not by Holy Tradition but by Madison Avenue, offers dozens of carefully tailored programs to meet the "needs" of individual believers.

Being consumer-oriented and consumer-driven, Christianity as self-help appeals to the selfishness of believers and caters to the cafeteria mentality of most American Christians. Instead of the Church transforming them, they are defining and transforming their churches, such that many of them appear not as houses of worship but as theatres, coffeehouses, and shopping malls. In this consumerist Christianity, Christ is there to "help" *me* with what *I* want. He is not there so that I may enter into His crucifixion and die and rise with Him, being transfigured into His likeness and becoming a partaker of the divine nature.

This kind of religion, which is focused on self-fulfillment rather than repentance, has also been successfully removed from the explicitly religious context and remarketed with great success. Perhaps the most successful example of this kind of religion is the spirituality offered by people like Oprah Winfrey, but what she offers is almost indistinguishable from what is sold by many televangelists and other mega-church pastors like Joel Osteen and Rick Warren, whose books are bestsellers and whose churches are packed with hordes of people looking to "feel better."

Another offspring of this breed of spirituality which is often crossbred with the others is called the **prosperity gospel,** or sometimes the "health and wealth gospel." This teaching has its origin in a strain of Calvinism that linked earthly prosperity with faith. For those Calvinists, a sign that you were among God's "elect" was that you enjoyed success in the earthly life. For prosperity gospel preachers, earthly success is directly linked to how much "faith" you have, which is often demonstrated by sending in donations to their ministry. The ostentatious and luxurious lives of such preachers are put forth as "proof" of their great faith.

Yet Christ's instruction to His Apostles and the witness of the saints is that those with true faith are often persecuted, poor, and hated by the world. For Orthodoxy, true faith is not measured by any of these things, certainly not by earthly riches. It also has nothing to do with being able to perform signs and wonders. True faith is a life of repentance of sins and participation in the grace-giving sacraments of the Church. True faith is humble, never making a show of anything, especially not miracles. When Jesus performed miracles, He used no emotionally manipulative music or over-anxious preaching. Indeed, He often sent everyone out of the room, and then after He was done told those He had healed not to spread the news to anyone.

Orthodoxy is marked by sobriety, not by emotional enthusiasm. It is also marked by a quite "ordinary" persistence in living the humble, consistent life of Christ, not by seeking out extraordinary experiences, especially supernatural ones. To the true believer, those experiences sometimes do come, but they are rare, and the example of the saints is that they are often suspicious of them. It is better accidentally to reject an angel by being overly vigilant than to embrace a demon through undiscerning enthusiasm.

DENOMINATIONAL FAMILIES AND MOVEMENTS

Many of the attitudes, doctrines, and practices we've discussed may broadly be included under the label *Evangelicalism*, but there is probably no one denomination, congregation, or even person who holds to all of them. Some may only have one or two elements of what we have described. Nevertheless, Evangelical Protestantism represents the second largest Christian grouping in America, second in size only to the Roman Catholic Church.

What almost all Evangelicals share is an emphasis on a "personal relationship with Christ." For most, this relationship has one goal: getting to heaven after death. For some, it may include other kinds of goals, such as earthly wealth, entertainment, or a sort of religious therapy. Evangelicals and Revivalists in general also share a commitment to evangelism, which, while laudable in itself, is probably largely the result of their lacking much in the way of a detailed spiritual life for the already converted believer. Thus, the convert, having been "saved," lacks much to do except to go out and help other people get "saved."

Now that we've looked at Revivalism in general, let's take a closer look at a few specific movements and denominational families that have their roots in Revivalism. The first two, Restorationism and Adventism, have their roots in the eighteenth century and took contrasting approaches to the central doctrine at issue in the Radical Reformation, ecclesiology.

Restorationism

Restorationism came out of the Revivalist movements in the late eighteenth and early nineteenth century in the United States, following the teachings of leaders Barton W. Stone and Thomas and Alexander Campbell and thus also known as the Stone-Campbellite Movement. The central idea of the Restorationist movement was that there is only one Church and that all Christian churches are somehow a part of it. Nevertheless, Restorationists believe in the Great Apostasy, though they would chart it as occurring over many centuries rather than shortly after the death of the Apostles. Restorationists ultimately believe that they are working toward the renewal and restoration of the New Testament Church and that the traditional creeds of historic Christianity only serve to divide rather than unite believers.

Ironically, Restorationism itself is divided. It is represented by several denominations, the largest of which are the Disciples of Christ and the Churches of Christ. Interestingly, like the Orthodox, the Churches of Christ regard themselves as being identical with the New Testament Church, seeing all other Christian groups as representing a schism from themselves. However, the Churches of Christ have no apostolic succession to back up this belief, which also contradicts their belief in the Great Apostasy. How can the Churches of Christ be the original New Testament Church if that New Testament Church completely fell away at some point in history? The only possible way to reconcile these beliefs is to believe that the Church has somehow been reincarnated after its death.

Ecclesiology for Restorationists is primarily understood in terms of organization rather than theology. Unity is a major theme, and this goal is to be accomplished through a common set of doctrines and practices, but without any hierarchy or denomination beyond the local congregation. Without the context of an episcopacy or denomination, it is easy to see why Restorationism split early on and remains divided. What was supposed to unite all Christians together divided even those in the movement.

Restorationists do have a number of things in common with the Orthodox, however, such as a belief in the necessity of baptism (although they do not baptize infants or believe that baptism accomplishes something in itself), holding communion frequently (though without a belief in the real presence), and (in many cases) *a cappella* music in church.

Despite these similarities, however, Restorationists generally hold to a view of the Bible in which silence is regarded as prohibition. Thus, many do not use instruments in music because they do not see them in the New Testament. They also do not see what the Orthodox see in the New Testament, namely, an ordained, sacramental clergy. Thus, while they do usually have a paid pastor, he is not called by any title and is not believed to have any special ministry different from anyone else in the congregation. Congregations do have elders and deacons, but they are administrative roles and have no special theological or sacramental significance.

Finally, the most significant criticism Orthodoxy has of the Restorationist movement is the same it has of all the children and grandchildren of the Radical Reformation: If the true Church was really lost at some point, how can you know that your version of it is a true restoration? Falling back on *sola scriptura* does not solve this problem, since all the descendants of the Reformation, divided into hundreds of denominations and tens of thousands of independent congregations, all claim to be simply "teaching the Bible."

There are three major Restorationist denominations or groupings in the United States: the Christian Church (Disciples of Christ), the Churches of Christ (non-instrumental), and the Churches of Christ (instrumental).

Adventism

The Adventist churches, the largest of which is the Seventh-day Adventist Church, are descendants of the Millerite movement of the 1840s. The Millerites, like the Radical Reformers and those who led the Revivalist movements, drew followers from across denominational lines, including Baptists like their leader William Miller, as well as Presbyterians, Methodists, and members of the Restorationist churches. Miller was a Baptist preacher from Low Hampton, New York, who calculated that Jesus Christ would return to earth on October 22, 1844. The Millerites had a handful of doctrines that made them distinct from their various denominational affiliations, but what united them was the common belief in the truth of Miller's calculation, which he claimed to have derived from prophetic passages in the Book of Daniel. Because Miller shared the now-common belief in a rejection of tradition and church authority, he believed that his method for reading the Bible was beyond question.

October 22, 1844, came and went, however, and there was no clear indication that Jesus had returned to earth. This came to be known as the "Great Disappointment," and most Millerites disbanded and returned to their various churches. Some, however, believed that Miller's calculations were correct but that his reading of Daniel was flawed. Instead of Christ returning to earth in 1844, He entered into an "inner sanctuary" in heaven, signaling the beginning of an "investigative judgment" of professed believers. Some believed that the October date in 1844 marked a "shut door" after which no true conversions to Christ could occur, although that has since been rejected.

It is out of this reorganized group of Millerites that the present-day Adventist churches were formed. They still believe the Second Coming is imminent, though they no longer set specific dates. One of the Adventist groups in particular believes that Christian worship should follow the Jewish pattern, and so they worship on Saturdays and are called "Seventh-day" Adventists, the largest of the Adventist denominations. (It should be noted that not all Adventists share identical theology.)

Besides the belief in the investigative judgment and observance of Saturday as the Christian holy day, some of the peculiar doctrines of Seventh-day Adventists include *soul sleep*, in which the human soul "sleeps" unconsciously between physical death and the final judgment, and *conditional immortality*, which means the wicked do not suffer eternally in the afterlife but are completely annihilated.

Adventists also are traditionally teetotalers, rejecting alcohol and tobacco use. They also encourage vegetarianism and avoidance of caffeine. Many fellow Protestants regard these emphases as "legalistic."

Seventh-day Adventist ecclesiology teaches that a "remnant" of true believers will be saved in the end. The true Church is therefore spread throughout all the world and probably across many denominations. Seventh-day Adventists completely accept the "invisible Church" ecclesiology of the Radical Reformation, that the true Church is ultimately invisible.

They also believe, however, that the Seventh-day Adventist Church is the true "visible Church," as elucidated in the writings of early-twentieth-century Adventist Ellen G. White, who is regarded as a prophet by many Adventists. Thus, Adventist ecclesiology represents something of a refinement of Radical Reformation ecclesiology. In this modern age of theological relativism, Adventists are often regarded as "exclusivist" because of this belief.

Seventh-day Adventists, like most Sabbatarians (those who practice Saturday worship rather than Sunday), date the Great Apostasy to about the year AD 135. St. Justin Martyr's description of liturgical Sunday worship in 160 is looked upon as evidence for this apostasy from the true faith.

The Holiness Movement

The Holiness Movement grew out of the Methodist Church in the mid-nineteenth century and represented another Pietistic revival, stressing the need for personal moral purity. Its central doctrine is entire sanctification, which is the idea that the Christian has the possibility for moral perfection in the earthly life, becoming free from all sinful desires. Followers believed that John Wesley's original teachings on Christian perfection had been eroded in the Methodist Church, and so they combined those teachings with the Revivalist techniques of the nineteenth century to create a new movement. Aside from its genesis in the Methodist Church, promoted initially by layman Phoebe Palmer, the movement also found success among some Congregationalists through the preaching of Charles G. Finney.

Although Wesley had taught the Christian life was more of a process, as does Orthodoxy, the Holiness Movement stressed Revivalist themes such as personal conversion and decision, with an increasing insistence on visible evidence of conversion. Through a series of Revivalist camp meetings, the movement began spreading throughout both North America and Great Britain. Tensions with Methodist leadership in the final decades of the nineteenth century eventually led to schism and the formation of new denominations. Holiness believers also were among the first to ordain women as clergy.

With a strong emphasis on the role of the Holy Spirit, the Holiness Movement eventually split into roughly two general groupings. The more conservative followers formed such denominations as the **Wesleyans,** the **Church of the Nazarene,** and the **Christian and Missionary Alliance.** The radical followers of the movement, those who placed a stronger emphasis on miraculous experiences, would form the various Pentecostal denominations, such as the Church of God and the Assemblies of God. A few Pentecostal groups, called Oneness Pentecostals, embraced the heresy of modalism (also called Sabellianism), the teaching that God is not three Persons, but rather one Person with three "modes."

Pentecostalism itself found its origins in the turn of the nineteenth and twentieth centuries. One of the more significant events in its history was the Azusa Street Revival, which took place in 1906 in Los Angeles and is generally regarded as the catalyst for modern Pentecostalism. At this revival and at other such events, believers would get together and pray for the "baptism of the Holy Spirit," which would often descend upon them with the kind of wild and unconventional behavior described before. Even otherwise conservative clergy came to the revival and were converted to its teachings. In the words of one observer at the time: "Proud, well-dressed preachers came to 'investigate'. Soon their high looks were replaced with wonder, then conviction comes, and very often you will find them in a short time wallowing on the dirty floor, asking God to forgive them and make them as little children" (quoted in Iain MacRobert's *The Black Roots and White Racism of Early Pentecostalism in the USA*).

The Mega-Church Movement

The twentieth century in particular saw the growth in America of so-called "non-denominationalism," which is essentially the most logical outcome of the commitment to congregationalism in church government. Non-denominational churches pride themselves on being completely autonomous organizations that answer to no one outside the local community. As the marketing approach to church growth took hold, especially in the 1980s, many believers left their old-fashioned churches to become part of what are now known as the "mega-churches."

The largest and most influential of these mega-churches in our own time is Willow Creek Community Church, located near Chicago. Willow Creek and churches like it practice a form of Evangelicalism deeply influenced by Revivalism. Worship music is typically upbeat and exciting, usually pop or rock-n-roll in style, often mixed with music from the Black Gospel tradition. There are typically dozens of programs to cater to the demographics that such churches are trying to attract. The whole church is designed with help from market research, making it consumer-driven. Often, this "seeker-sensitive" marketing looks at the dominant demographic in an area and works to cater to them, which may make such congregations demographically imbalanced, filled for instance with many thirty-somethings but not very many elderly.

Interestingly, in 2007 Willow Creek itself came out with a study of its success over the years, and they discovered that the most dissatisfied members of their congregation were not those who were the most disengaged. Rather, they were those who were most involved. That is, those whom they regarded by their own measures as spiritually mature were those most likely to begin to move away from the church. While Willow Creek is busy retooling its programs to try to "address" this "need," the problem is inherent to Revivalism itself—it has a strong emphasis on personal conversion, but without any historical Christian tradition, it has very little to offer for the long haul. All it can do is keep adding new self-help programs to help believers "cope."

What Orthodoxy offers, by contrast, is participation in the divine Energies of God. That's not very "seeker-sensitive," but it is the path to Christlikeness, communion with the Holy Trinity.

Dispensationalism and Covenant Theology

One of the theological movements arising out of the nineteenth century is Dispensationalism. The central idea behind this theology is that God divided history into various segments called *dispensations*. In each of these dispensations, man's relationship with God is practiced differently. Thus, what it meant to be "saved" for the ancient Jews is different from what it means for Christians today. Dispensationalists would probably not put it that way, however, instead saying that each dispensation is rather an "emphasis" on some particular aspect of obedience to God. They would teach that all people still can be saved only by grace through faith, although what that looks like differs with each dispensation.

Dispensationalism often is very much interested in the end times, as it sees all of history as a series of prophecies leading to those final days. Theological manuals on Dispensationalism often include vast series of charts and drawings, usually incorporating apocalyptic imagery from the Books of Daniel and Revelation. A number of Dispensationalists have tried their hand at predicting the date of the end of the world.

For many of these believers, Judaism is in some sense a legitimate religion. This theology has strongly influenced much of American Evangelicalism and has had an influence on American foreign policy. Some of these Christians regard the formation of the modern secular state of Israel in 1948 as a fulfillment of biblical prophecy, and thus believe that America should do everything we can to support Israel against its enemies.

From the Orthodox point of view, any attempt to superimpose a complex system onto the Bible and onto history in general will doubtless lead to false conclusions. Rather, what we see revealed in every time and place is Christ. The Old Testament itself is to be read in the light of Christ. We can see a gradual process of God revealing Himself throughout the Old Testament, finally being fully revealed in Christ; but the Bible itself, the Apostles, and the tradition they taught do not include a system of discrete historical periods.

Further, Judaism as it is now practiced is essentially synagogue Pharisaism, the one sect that survived the destruction of the Jerusalem Temple in AD 70. It is not even a direct successor to ancient Judaism, since the priesthood did not survive. Nevertheless, all forms of modern Judaism are illegitimate in God's eyes, since the New Israel is the Church. Orthodoxy has always taught that all of God's promises to Israel now belong to the Church.

Some believers influenced by Dispensationalism have formed groups known as Messianic Judaism, which have certain Christian beliefs but also practice some Jewish rituals. They may often reinterpret classic Christian doctrine in Jewish terms. Instead of reading the Old Testament in light of the New, they tend to read the New Testament in light of the Old. This movement is essentially a revival of the ancient Judaizing heresy. Interestingly, though, some Messianic Jews have become Orthodox Christians (such as Fr. James Bernstein, author of *Surprised by Christ* [Conciliar Press, 2008], who was once a prominent member of Jews for Jesus), probably finding in Orthodoxy the answer to their longing for historical roots.

A related theological outlook arising in the twentieth century is covenant theology, which is generally associated with Presbyterianism. This theology teaches that God has set up two covenants. The first was with Adam, who received death because he disobeyed. The second, covering both Jews and Christians, was made with Christ by grace. In Christ, God's covenant with Israel was transferred to the Church, and Judaism is now cut off from the covenant because of its rejection of Christ.

While Orthodoxy agrees that the Church is the New Israel, there truly has only ever been one path to salvation for mankind, one covenant, and that is in Christ. The Fathers sometimes even say that the Incarnation would have happened even if Adam had not sinned. Therefore, the possibility of union with God in Christ was presupposed even at the creation of Adam.

Liberalism and Fundamentalism

It is common in our own time to hear the words *liberalism* and *fundamentalism* bandied about in discussions of religion. What is usually not known, however, is that these words have historical bases and usage. Liberalism in Protestantism (also called Modernism) is generally characteristic of the mainline denominations (Methodists, Episcopalians, some Presbyterians and Lutherans, etc.), and it is the direct result of eighteenth- and nineteenth-century rationalism. With rationalism's emphasis on human reason, coupled with archaeology and studies of the variant textual manuscripts of the Bible, many Christians in these denominations came to doubt the authenticity and authority of the Scripture itself. This doubt had a devastating effect for many believers, since their faith was based on *sola scriptura*. If Christian faith is based exclusively on the Bible, and if the Bible is shown somehow to be lacking or false or mistaken, then why should I believe in Christ at all?

For some believers, this question led to a loss of faith. For others, their faith radically changed. The Bible came to be understood as an interesting ancient text with many good teachings, but it wasn't to be taken too seriously. What really mattered was social justice and living a moral life, a view which is often called the "social gospel." Traditional doctrines, especially those depending on miracles such as the Virgin Birth, were to be held only with suspicion or perhaps discarded entirely.

One reaction against biblical liberalism began in the early-twentieth-century Presbyterian Church in the United States and came to be called Fundamentalism. The Fundamentalists taught that there were certain "fundamentals" of faith that had to be believed in order for a believer to be a legitimate Christian. After a series of heresy trials, the Fundamentalists eventually broke with the Liberals and formed a new denomination, the Orthodox Presbyterian Church. The name Fundamentalist was used until at least the late 1970s by many Protestant Christians, not just Presbyterians, who believed that you had to profess certain doctrines in order to be a real Christian. Thus, while Fundamentalism originally referred to the formation of a Presbyterian orthodoxy, nowadays it means something entirely different. It's typically quite vague in usage, but probably usually means "anyone who is more serious than I am about religion," especially if they have a gun.

The Next Pietism

In the *Dune* science fiction series by Frank Herbert, there is a saying which accurately describes a repeated storyline within the books: "Every revolution carries within it the seeds of its own destruction." In each of the books, a revolution of the whole society comes to fruition at the end. In the book that follows, that revolution has become the "establishment," and a new revolution begins to form which overthrows the new establishment. This same dynamic seems to be at work in much of Protestantism, especially in the spiritual children of Revivalism.

In the past several years, another set of movements has begun. What began in the eighteenth and nineteenth centuries as a new, exciting, unconventional movement has now become the Evangelical establishment, and new theological revolutionaries are even now beginning to set the stage for the next set of doctrinal innovations. These movements go by various kinds of names, but one label which has been getting some attention is the **emergent church.**

If you try to study what it is these "emergents" believe and do, your head will spin. There is absolutely no unified theological vision that goes along with this label. Even when looking at the writings of individual believers, it is almost impossible to figure out what each person believes. As an example, I offer to you the subtitle of an emergent book by author Brian D. McLaren. His book, entitled *A Generous Orthodoxy*, is of course quite generous but hardly Orthodox, at least not by Orthodox standards. The subtitle of his book is, "Why I am a missional, evangelical, post/protestant, liberal/conservative, mystical/poetic, biblical, charismatic/contemplative, fundamentalist/Calvinist, Anabaptist/

Anglican, Methodist, catholic, green, incarnational, depressed-yet-hopeful, emergent, unfinished Christian." I must confess that I am at a loss as to what that means.

In any event, we can say a few things about the so-called emergent movement. It is strongly anti-establishment. Emergents have been leaving established church communities in droves, often setting up new communities in people's homes. They tend to value being "on the edge," not just in terms of their theology but also in their worship. Emergent worship may include liturgical elements that a believer found in an interesting book, and it may also include in the same service a bewildering electric light show and emotionally charged, "mystical" music. Where all of this is leading is hard to say.

Mainstream Evangelicals often look at emergents as heretical, especially as new theological ideas are gaining currency in such circles. One such idea is called **open theism,** which is at its core the teaching that not even God can know the future, because the future doesn't exist yet. This doctrine is based on the erroneous assumption that God experiences time the same way we do. Theology and Christian life are usually not expressed in terms of Creed, but rather of "conversation." Whether that conversation will ever come to any conclusions has yet to be seen.

Dedication to doctrine among emergents is weak, and emergents see themselves as more of a "movement" than a denomination, often crossing denominational lines. In this, we can see yet another resurgence of the Pietistic spirit. Emergent Christians are even more oriented toward the smorgasbord approach to religion than the established Revivalist churches from which they came. They are often quite interested in tradition, but almost never willing to adopt a tradition in its wholeness, preferring rather to select certain attractive elements of tradition to incorporate into their hybrid spirituality. Emergents are, interestingly, more open to physical and mystical elements in worship than many of their dualistic forebears.

At the very least, this movement is an indication that there is a dissatisfaction with the Revivalist mainstream, particularly its perceived commercial aspect. There is an opportunity here for the Orthodox to meet these believers where they are, to discuss with them their criticisms of mainstream Evangelicalism, and then to show them how different Orthodoxy is and how it answers their deepest longings.

CONCLUSIONS

Most of the converts to the Orthodox Church in recent years have come pre-cisely from the churches influenced the most by Revivalism. When these folks begin to set aside their dualistic biases and consider that there might be a physi-cal side to being spiritual, they are naturally led to ask certain kinds of ques-tions: What is the Church? Can I locate it? Does it have authority?

We can also observe in recent years a revival of interest in Christian his-tory. The success of books like *The Da Vinci Code* (a work of fiction, not fact, as any first-semester student of church history could tell you) is testament to this interest. The newness of the American frontier has worn off over the past cen-tury, and many Christians are now turning toward a desire for rootedness and steadfastness. The highest rates of growth in American Christianity are among the groups that have a strong sense of unchanging doctrine, while those that embrace theological liberalism and pluralism are seeing the biggest defections.

It is true, of course, that groups that at one time might have been called "Fundamentalist" offer a solid doctrinal core, and those groups are seeing growth. Yet when one examines their history and the rest of Christian history, one finds that apparently solid doctrine is usually no more than a hundred years old at best. What Orthodoxy offers to such seekers is twenty centuries of wit-ness that there is one Christian faith, given by Christ to the Apostles and pre-served throughout history. All are welcome to come and see.

Six

Non-Mainstream Christians

MANY GODS, MANY CHRISTS

For false christs and false prophets will rise and show great signs and wonders to deceive, if possible, even the elect.

(Matthew 24:24)

In the preceding chapters, we examined the doctrines of other Christians, from Roman Catholics to the churches of the Magisterial and Radical Reformations to the churches of Revivalism. With the vast majority of them, we saw how we shared certain basic beliefs, such as belief in the Holy Trinity and in the incarnate God-man Jesus Christ. The details of how those beliefs get worked out are certainly crucial, but there is still some basic common ground.

In this chapter, we will examine the beliefs of groups that call themselves "Christian," but are largely regarded as non-Christians by most of the groups we have already covered. Mainstream Christians may look upon these people as "cults" or "heretics." This rejection of the "Christian" label for these groups by other Christians is largely based on these non-mainstream groups' rejection of the traditional dogmas of the Holy Trinity and the nature of Jesus Christ as professed by the mainstream. While the Orthodox Church stands with the mainstream Christian communions in affirming that these traditional dogmas are necessary elements of Christian faith, we differ with them on what else it means to be truly Christian.

One of the things we will see as we look at these various communions is that once basic dogma is discarded, the whole theological world can radically shift for a believer. While Orthodoxy believes that traditional Triadology and Christology are not the only elements of Christian dogma, the Church regards these dogmas in particular as anchors which hold fast, inform, and shape all other parts of Christian theology and therefore spiritual life. It is for this reason that the beliefs and practices of these non-mainstream denominations often look and sound so different from those of other Christians.

With most mainstream Christian groups, we can believe that we are probably worshiping or at least talking about the same God, though with some extreme doctrines such as Calvinism, that commonality is decidedly strained. With the communions we will examine in this chapter, however, it is almost impossible to regard our faiths as being even remotely aimed in the same direction. That is the reason that when a believer comes to the Orthodox Church from one of these groups, even if they had been baptized before within them, their baptism is in no way accepted by the Orthodox, and they are usually received into Orthodoxy with the full conversion process normally reserved for non-Christians.

This approach may seem unfair, especially considering that the foundation for these non-mainstream groups is often the same as that of most mainstream denominations—that is, their source of authority is yet another individual claiming to have the corner on biblical interpretation or revelation from God. Yet if we look at the practices of even the ancient Church, we will find that an uneven approach has always been taken within Orthodoxy when receiving converts from other faiths. St. Basil the Great in the fourth century, for instance, says that certain kinds of heretics should be baptized and chrismated, others should only be chrismated, and still others are received solely through profession of faith. These distinctions do not reveal an arrogance on the part of the Church, but rather a willingness to try to work with whatever can be found in a converting believer that can be adapted to Orthodoxy. With some believers, there is more than with others. Even for those who are clearly non-Christians, such as Jews or Muslims, catechesis will vary. A Jew is closer to us than is a Muslim, for instance.

Keeping this method in mind, that the Church is always in search of the means to bring about the full blossoming of truth in every human person, let us now examine the particulars of our differences from non-mainstream Christian groups.

UNITARIAN UNIVERSALISTS

Unitarianism is the teaching that God is not a Trinity of divine Persons, but rather that He is absolutely one divine Person. This belief itself actually had proponents among early heretics, most especially Sabellius, who taught that Father, Son, and Holy Spirit were simply "modes" of a single Person of God. The Unitarian Universalist Association as a religious denomination was founded in 1961. Nevertheless, despite the modern denomination's relatively short history, its origins actually lie in the seventeenth-century Radical Reformation, which produced theologians referred to as Unitarians.

A number of Unitarians were produced during the Protestant Reformation, though they did not form any lasting denominations. In the mid-seventeenth century in England, John Biddle published a number of Unitarian tracts and held private meetings in London. American Unitarianism, which is the source of the modern denomination, began most clearly in the late eighteenth century with the formation of King's Chapel in Boston in 1785, adapting a form of the Episcopal liturgy according to Unitarian doctrine. In 1825 a denomination was formed, called the American Unitarian Association. The early nineteenth century saw Unitarianism adopted in a number of Congregational churches, most especially in New England.

By the end of the nineteenth century, American Unitarianism had been heavily influenced by Enlightenment rationalism and began to reject a number of traditional Christian doctrines and practices, even beyond the repudiation of Trinitarian theology. Unitarian theology came to be extremely liberal in its outlook and began to look more toward science for doctrinal guidance, as well as formally recognizing other religions as being true.

While Unitarianism was developing in the United States, Universalism also was gaining ground, particularly among Christians of the Pietist and Anabaptist movements coming out of the Radical Reformation. The year 1778 saw the first convention of what became the Universalist Church of America. The essential distinctive teaching of Universalism is that, because it is God's will that all should be saved (2 Peter 3:9), then all will eventually be saved, no matter what they do or believe in this life. This teaching had a few adherents in the ancient Church, as well, whose belief was summed up with the term *apokatastasis*, the "recapitulation" of all things in Christ, even Satan.

In 1961, the American Unitarian Association and the Universalist Church of America merged to form the Unitarian Universalist Association. It is not a denomination in a traditional sense but rather an association of congregations. The association has no ability to speak for all of them as a whole. With the merging of two denominations that were historically Christian but dedicated to radical theology, the association has now evolved into a religious group without any doctrine.

Their website states:

> Unitarian Universalism is a liberal religion that encompasses many faith traditions. Unitarian Universalists include people who identify as Christians, Jews, Buddhists, Hindus, Pagans, Atheists, Agnostics, Humanists, and others. As there is no official Unitarian Universalist creed, Unitarian Universalists are free to search for truth on many paths. To quote the Rev. Marta Flanagan, "We uphold the free search for truth. We will not be bound by a statement of belief. We do not ask anyone to subscribe to a creed. We say ours is a non-creedal religion. Ours is a free faith." Although we uphold shared principles, individual Unitarian Universalists have varied beliefs about everything from scripture to rituals to God.

The "shared principles" of UUs (as they are often called) amount to little more than a statement of basic human rights such as one might find in the American Constitution, as well as affirmations such as "respect for the interdependent web of all existence of which we are a part." Many UUs are former members of other churches who enjoy the social, ethical, and charitable aspects of religious life but are less interested in traditional religious questions such as salvation.

Despite the lack of doctrine among UUs, they do still have some rituals, though of course these vary widely from congregation to congregation. One example is "Flower Communion," in which each member brings a flower to the meeting and puts it into a vase. These flowers are "consecrated" by a minister during the service. At the end, each person walks away with a flower different from the one he brought with him. Believers are encouraged to interpret this ritual however they like. In a similar ritual, UUs may each bring some water with them from various locations. The water is then combined together and used for blessings.

With such an immensely broad definition of Unitarian Universalism, it is hard to know where we might have commonality with the group as a whole. The Orthodox Church may certainly have things in common with individual believers, but since the whole UU religion seems to be dedicated to the notion that there is no absolute, universal truth, Orthodox Christians find it to be antithetical to our most basic beliefs. Although the Bible, for instance, may be studied by UUs, it is regarded as full of "mythical and legendary" material and not as a representative of the truth in any binding sense. There are absolutely no set beliefs in the Unitarian Universalist Association.

There are about 800,000 Unitarian Universalists in the world, mostly in the United States.

SWEDENBORGIANS

Emanuel Swedenborg was a Swedish scientist and philosopher born in 1688. His father Jesper Swedberg was a professor of theology and later became the Lutheran bishop of Skara in Sweden. Swedenborg himself was gifted with a brilliant mind and mathematical ability, and in his writings anticipated many scientific hypotheses and inventions, such as nebular and magnetic theory, the machine-gun, and the airplane. In 1716, he was appointed by the Swedish king to a post on the Swedish Board of Mines.

In the 1740s, Swedenborg began claiming to have direct contact with angels and the spiritual world, partly in dreams and visions, but also in his normal waking life. He believed through these revelations that God was sending him on a mission to make the truth known to mankind. The vehicle for this mission was the so-called New Church, proposed not as a new denomination but rather as a fraternity of like-minded believers joining across denominational lines (much like the Pietist movements of the Radical Reformation). In 1747 he resigned his position on the Board of Mines and began intensively studying the Bible, spending the rest of his life writing detailed defenses of his teachings while living in Sweden, the Netherlands, and finally in London.

Swedenborgianism initially found supporters among Anglican clergy, but it was five ex-Wesleyan preachers who worked to create an actual Swedenborgian denomination in 1787, then called the New Jerusalem Church. The first American congregation was formed in Baltimore in 1792. A smaller, separate body of Swedenborgians was formed in 1890 and based in Bryn Athyn, Pennsylvania, called the General Church of New Jerusalem. Various other bodies of Swedenborgians exist in other parts of the world.

Swedenborg's religious system was based on what he called a "doctrine of correspondence" between the physical and spiritual worlds. The spiritual world consists of groups of deceased humans who together constitute one single great human being. Christ is the greatest manifestation of humanity, but did not atone for mankind's sins on the Cross. His mission was not to redeem from sin but rather to show the nature of spiritual life and to provide an example of it.

Swedenborg's theology is Unitarian at its core, teaching that God is a single divine Person, and that Father, Son, and Holy Spirit are "aspects" of God just as soul, body, and activity are aspects of a human person. In Jesus, Swedenborgians see Father, Son, and Holy Spirit, and He is regarded as a "manifestation" of God, "the divine made flesh," whose Second Coming has already occurred and is ongoing in a spiritual sense.

Mankind consists of spirits clothed in material bodies. "Spiritual bodies" live on after death. The afterlife is determined by our behavior in this life, not through God passing a judgment on us, but through our own choices. The final "judgment" is essentially self-realization after death; those who die are grouped in the afterlife with other people with the same kind of spiritual attitude. In heaven, all those who are married in this life will continue to have the same spouse, and some singles may get married in heaven.

Obviously the Orthodox differ from Swedenborgians on major doctrines, such as the nature of God and Christ. We also believe in a physical, material resurrection for all mankind, because the body is an essential component of human personhood. In general, Swedenborgianism has a tendency to "spiritualize" (that is, to dematerialize) the spiritual life, a tendency Orthodoxy does not share, seeing Christian life as involving both the soul and the body, as well as the whole material world.

Swedenborgians are encouraged to focus on the meanings of dreams, as well as on prayer and meditation. This mystical tradition often sets believers apart from mainstream Western Christianity, though it is a point of contact with Orthodoxy, which also has a strong mystical tradition (though not in the dualistic, anti-material sense held by Swedenborgians). Orthodox Christians also share with Swedenborgians the belief that there is an "inner" meaning to the Bible, but our understanding of that meaning is never one divorced from the concrete events of sacred history and their representation to us, most especially in the sacraments.

World membership is claimed at only about 65,000, and membership in the U.S. has been in decline since its peak in the 1850s. Some sources put their membership at about 25,000 to 30,000. While Swedenborgianism is relatively unknown to most Christians, some Swedenborgians have gained fame in America, such as John Chapman ("Johnny Appleseed") and Helen Keller.

MORMONS

It was the year 1820, the midpoint of the Second Great Awakening, one of the great Revivalist movements in the United States, and in the town of Palmyra, New York, a fourteen-year-old farm boy began to wonder which of the many Christian denominations was the true faith. The part of western New York where the boy lived was referred to as the "Burned-over District," since it had so many times "caught on fire" for God in revival. Although the boy's family had little to do with organized religion, they often claimed to have received visions and prophecies from God. There is also some evidence that members of the family, including his father, may have used divining rods to try to locate buried treasure and other hard-to-find objects. The boy himself may also have attended some Methodist revival meetings. In the midst of this religious atmosphere, one can see how a teenager would be confused about what was really true.

The boy later claimed that the answer to his pondering came in the miraculous appearance to him in a vision of God and Jesus, who told him that all Christian denominations had fallen away from the true faith and that it would be restored in time. Three years later, at the age of seventeen, he claimed to see a vision of an angel named Moroni, who told him where to find a set of golden plates buried in a hillside. Unearthing these plates, along with a pair of special seeing stones that allowed him to read the plates, as they had been inscribed with writing in an ancient language, the boy reported that he had discovered ancient texts from long-forgotten Native American tribes. The boy's name was Joseph Smith, and what he claimed to have found was the Book of Mormon. The religion founded on this discovery came to be called Mormonism, and Smith, along with other Mormon leaders, is believed by Mormons to have been a prophet.

Initially, Smith said that Moroni would not allow him to remove his archaeological find from the hillside, but he visited a few times over the next few years. During this time, Smith himself may have gotten involved in divining the location of buried treasure and other items. Finally, in 1827, when he was twenty-one, Smith was permitted to remove the plates, and he began the process of translating them by using the seeing stones buried with them. In the process of this translation, Smith would often put his face into his hat, along with the seeing stones, and he would dictate the translation into English to various scribes, claiming that he was not permitted to continue dictating until the scribes had correctly inscribed his exact translation, word for word and letter for letter.

In 1830, Smith officially founded his church in Manchester, New York, calling it simply the Church of Christ. In time, in addition to his "translation" work, he came to author contributions to two books, *Doctrine and Covenants* and *The Pearl of Great Price*. These books, together with an edited version of the Bible and the Book of Mormon, are regarded by the Mormons as sacred scripture. Claiming to restore the true Christian Church after centuries of apostasy, Mormonism is another of the Restorationist movements coming out of the nineteenth century.

In 1843, Smith said he received a revelation from God sanctioning polygamy, which he referred to as "plural marriage." Putting this revelation into practice, Smith himself may have had as many as forty-four wives over the course of seventeen years. Despite being a revelation of supposedly eternal value, polygamy was later repudiated by most Mormons in 1890, probably largely as a result of pressure from the federal government, which refused to recognize Utah as a state unless it outlawed the practice. These Mormons believe that plural marriage will be restored in heaven, however.

There have actually been dozens of Mormon denominations since the initial group was founded in 1830, but the primary one is the one led immediately after Smith by Brigham Young, who acted as Smith's right-hand man and commanded the majority of followers after Smith was killed by a mob in 1844. This main group is called the Church of Jesus Christ of Latter-Day Saints (LDS).

The Mormons believe in the Holy Trinity, but they regard the Father, the Son, and the Holy Spirit as three separate "gods" who are united in purpose, which they refer to as the "Godhead" (which is an Orthodox Christian term, as well, though Orthodox use it with very different meaning). Unlike the God of Orthodox Christians, these gods are not uncreated. In fact, the Father who created our world was once human but gradually became god over time. (For a time, the Mormon church taught that Adam is God the Father.) As Joseph Smith said, "God Himself was once as we are now, and is an exalted man." Another Mormon leader coined the saying, "As man is, God once was; as God is, man may become." This is the goal of life as a Mormon, to become a god. An elevated Mormon will also get to father many children and to create his own world, beginning the cycle of creation over again.

Jesus is therefore of course "god," but he was born from sexual reproduction just as every other "god" was. He is a "spirit child" of the Heavenly Father who created our world. Another one of these "spirit children" is Lucifer, that is, Satan, who opposed his older brother Jesus. Interestingly, though, we are all considered "spirit children" of the Father, though this was in our "premortal life." So, yes, Satan is taught to be Jesus' brother, but he is our brother, too. And the Father, who has a physical body, has had several wives, and Mary's giving birth to Jesus is taught to be the result of intercourse with the Father, though it is defined as a "virgin birth" because it was intercourse with God and not with a mortal man.

As we have seen, Mormon doctrine concerning the Trinity is radically different from Orthodoxy, because Mormons are polytheists, while Orthodoxy is monotheistic. Further, Mormon soteriology (doctrine of salvation) sounds similar to the Orthodox doctrine of *theosis*, but in Orthodoxy, man does not become an almighty god, but rather participates in and becomes transformed by the one and only God. The key problem in all Mormon theology in general is the failure to distinguish between the created and the uncreated.

Like the Orthodox, Mormons believe in and practice baptism, regarding it as a normal part of salvation. Yet for Mormons, baptism is so absolutely essential that they believe it is utterly impossible to ascend in the afterlife without it. Thus, Mormons may practice what is called baptism for the dead, a proxy baptism for someone who has died. By this practice, Mormons believe they are converting people to Mormonism. Their concern for all their ancestors becoming Mormon is the reason for the strong interest in genealogy. Mormons are researching their family trees so that they can retroactively convert their ancestry to Mormonism.

Mormons also believe in ongoing revelation, even if it sometimes contradicts revelations previously preached by Mormon leaders. Aside from the about-face on plural marriage, Mormonism has also changed its teaching on race. It used to be impossible, for instance, for black men to become part of the Mormon priesthood, but that teaching was later reversed. Even the Book of Mormon itself has been revised over the years. Most of the thousands of revisions involve minor errors or idiosyncrasies in grammar and spelling, but other more major changes have been made. This would not be much of a problem if Joseph Smith hadn't claimed that his translation itself was divinely inspired, even to the point of requiring that the scribes taking dictation from him had to get it right before God would let him continue. Many of the changes Mormons have made in their teachings over the years have been covered up by LDS leaders.

There are many problems with the Book of Mormon even aside from its revision history. For one thing, whole passages are copied word-for-word from the King James Version of the Bible. Many other portions have language similar to that of the King James Bible but without the grammar and usage that were correct in early seventeenth-century England. (In other words, it is an imitation of the King James, but badly done.)

Further, the text claims that Jews came to North America in ancient times and that Jesus came here after His resurrection. Detailed information is given about various ancient civilizations that supposedly existed in North America. It is also claimed that the golden plates from which the Book of Mormon was translated were written in a script known as "Reformed Egyptian." Yet there is not one manuscript, not one shred of archaeological evidence, nor any corroboration from any non-Mormon source that might back up such claims, nor even the existence of such a language. There are even strong arguments that elements of the Book of Mormon were plagiarized from other books published shortly before it (including a novel titled *A Manuscript Found*, by ex-preacher Solomon Spalding).

Aside from these criticisms, there is good evidence that many Mormon symbols, teachings, and even ceremonies were adapted from Freemasonry. In fact, the mob that assaulted and killed Smith in 1844 may have been inspired by Freemasons who felt betrayed that Smith, a member of the Freemasons along with a number of other Mormon leaders, had revealed their secrets to non-Masons.

Mormonism is currently growing by nearly 250,000 people every year. The Mormon community tends to be strongly moral and friendly, and the Mormon missionaries who de-emphasize the more controversial teachings of the religion help to facilitate its spread. Many converts are unaware of a good many of the things we have mentioned.

The main Mormon denomination, the Church of Jesus Christ of Latter-Day Saints, currently claims over 13 million members, spread over about 175 countries. All Mormon men are expected to spend two years of their lives as missionaries, at their own expense. There are currently about 53,000 such missionaries in the world—about one for every 245 Mormons. If the Orthodox Church commissioned missionaries at the same rate, we would have about one million missionaries preaching the true Christian faith.

CHRISTADELPHIANS

The Christadelphians were originally called the Thomasites for their founder, John Thomas, an English doctor who started the group in America in 1848. The word *Christadelphians* itself, meaning "Christ's brothers," was Thomas's substitute for *Christians*, a term he rejected, since he believed that the traditional associations with the term actually constituted an apostasy from the true teachings of Jesus. Thomas himself claimed to have the original teachings of Jesus and His first disciples.

Thomas joined the Restorationist movement of the Stone-Campbellites, but eventually his insistence on his own doctrine led him into a series of fierce debates with Alexander Campbell. As a result, Thomas was "disfellowshipped" by the movement and left to strike out on his own. He became associated with some of the Adventist Millerite groups of the nineteenth century and was even baptized three times during a period of personal doctrinal evolution, each time renouncing his previous beliefs. He eventually settled down as a preacher in Philadelphia and formulated his teachings based on a philosophical reading of the Bible. He said he was revealing its true teachings, not through any special revelation given to him by God, but rather through careful study of the Bible, which he saw as the exclusive record of God's revelation to mankind.

Thomas also preached in Richmond, Virginia, and New York City, especially targeting Jews, because he placed great emphasis on Christ's fulfillment of the Law of Moses. He and his followers became known during this time as the Royal Association of Believers. Thomas later traveled to the South in the 1860s, concerned that the Civil War was dividing believers. Because he wanted his followers to be exempt from military service on religious grounds, it was at this time that he officially formed an organization and coined the term *Christadelphians* to refer to his followers. He later traveled to England, preaching there as well.

Christadelphians, who refer to themselves as a "Bible-based community," are Unitarian, rejecting the doctrine of the Trinity and teaching that only the Father is God. They believe that the name *Holy Spirit* simply refers to the power of God the Father in the world. (The Orthodox identify this power as the energies of God, which are uncreated and common to all three Persons of the Trinity.) Christadelphians reject the divinity of Jesus Christ, because of the philosophical contradiction between God being immortal and the death of Jesus on the Cross. They also believe that Jesus' temptation by the devil proves that He is not divine, since temptation without the possibility of sin is supposedly meaningless. From this basic attitude toward God and the nature of Jesus Christ, we can see that Christadelphians are strongly committed to philosophical categories to determine their theology.

Even though they teach that Jesus was only a man, Christadelphians believe that He was the Son of God, was sinless, and that God raised Him from the dead and made Him the mediator between God and man. Even though human beings are not *naturally* immortal (a position the Orthodox agree with), Jesus was granted immortality by God. Jesus, instead of being the God-man as in Orthodox doctrine, thus occupies a sort of Neoplatonic position as an intermediary between the divine world and the human, though without truly being part of the divine.

Christadelphians teach that salvation is possible through belief in the Bible and obedience to its commandments, by accepting Christ's sacrifice on the Cross and being baptized (which is only for adults). Those who die without having done this will eventually be annihilated, because immortality is a gift only to the righteous. By contrast, Orthodoxy teaches that God sustains all human beings in immortality whether they accept Him or not, and salvation is about much more than simply belief, obedience, and acceptance. Salvation is rather a whole life of communion with God and participation in the life of the Holy Trinity, progressing infinitely through all eternity.

The devil is seen by Christadelphians not as a supernatural being, a fallen angel as in Orthodoxy, but rather as a symbol used by the Bible to refer to the sinful human nature. Christadelphians also do not tithe, because they believe tithing was limited only to supporting the levitical priesthood in the Old Testament. They believe Christians are not the New Israel but are rather grafted into the ethnic Israel, which remains the People of God. At the end of time, Jesus will come again to earth and set up a literal worldwide kingdom with its capital at Jerusalem.

All of their teachings they claim come directly from the Bible, and they believe that a process of debate and studious inquiry into the Scriptures will lead the believer into becoming a Christadelphian on his own. Christadelphians use the same canon of Scripture as most Protestants and describe themselves as a "community of Bible students."

John Thomas's followers have never been many in number. Christadelphians gather in fully autonomous local congregations called *ecclesias*, often grouped into associating fellowships, but have no denomination as such and publish no official membership figures. They also have no professional clergy. Their numbers are estimated at about 50,000 worldwide.

CHRISTIAN SCIENCE

Christian Science is the system of religious belief of the Church of Christ, Scientist. The denomination was founded in 1879 by Mary Baker Eddy, a New Hampshire native raised with Calvinist beliefs. From her youth she suffered from various ailments, but believed she had been cured of them by a hypnotist. About a year after this cure, however, she suffered a relapse. In 1866, at the age of 45, she said she experienced instantaneous physical healing while reading the account of the cure of the paralytic in Matthew 9. After this, Eddy claimed to have discovered the spiritual law and the science behind the healing work of Jesus.

In 1875, she published the first edition of her book dedicated to teaching her discoveries, entitled *Science and Health*, expanded in 1883 to include another work, *Key to the Scriptures*. Four years later, the Church of Christ, Scientist, was incorporated in Boston and became the "Mother Church" of a new denomination with Mrs. Eddy as its chief pastor. In 1895, she published *The Manual of the Mother Church* to organize its workings.

The single most distinctive teaching of Christian Science is the belief in the unreality of the material world. For Christian Scientists, the only thing truly real is the spiritual world. Materiality is an illusion. As a result, if someone is suffering from some sickness, all they need to do to be cured is to realize that their sickness is just an illusion. All evil can be destroyed simply by becoming aware of the power and love of God. Seeking medical treatment is the result of a lack of faith. Heaven itself is a "divine state of mind." Mrs. Eddy once summarized her central teachings with what is called "The Scientific Statement of Being": "There is no life, truth, intelligence, nor substance in matter. All is infinite Mind and its infinite manifestation, for God is All-in-all. Spirit is immortal Truth; matter is mortal error. Spirit is the real and eternal; matter is the unreal and temporal. Spirit is God, and man is His image and likeness. Therefore man is not material; he is spiritual."

Christian Science accepts the historical accounts of the birth, life, death, and resurrection of Jesus, but Mrs. Eddy drew a distinction between Jesus as a man and the "Christ" which is the divinity He manifested. Jesus is thus "divine" but not God. God Himself is called "Father-Mother," and the Holy Spirit is equivalent to the "divine science," that is, Christian Science teaching. Jesus is still regarded as God's Son. Although Eddy rejected traditional Trinitarian theology as polytheism, there is in her teachings a semi-Trinitarian side to God, defined as "Truth, Life, and Love." God may also be referred to by other terms, such as Principle, Soul, Mind, and Spirit.

Christian Science religious services are quite simple, consisting mainly of readings from the Bible and from *Science and Health*. Also included are hymns, the recitation of the Lord's Prayer, and silent prayer. There are twenty-six official set topics for the "lesson-sermon," which are cycled twice throughout the year. In a year with fifty-three Sundays, one of them is used three times. These lesson-sermons are used at every congregation and have titles such as, "Are Sin, Disease and Death Real?" and "Is the Universe, Including Man, Evolved by Atomic Force?"

From the Orthodox point of view, Christian Science is a combination of multiple ancient heresies: most especially gnostic dualism, with its denial of the material world; Nestorianism, with its radical disjunction between Jesus and Christ; Monarchianism, which denied the Trinity; and Pneumatomachianism, with its denial of the divinity of the Holy Spirit.

Christian Scientists have neither ordained clergy nor sacraments. Baptism and Holy Communion are thought of in purely spiritual—that is, non-material—terms. The primary focus in Christian Science is on spiritual healing, referred to on the Mother Church's website as a "healing and educational system." While many members will testify as to the reality of the healing powers of their religious methods, they have never been corroborated outside the denomination.

From the Orthodox point of view, the dualistic anti-materialism of Christian Science is simply delusion and a denial of God's creation. Creation exists in both visible and invisible elements, both material and immaterial, in an eternal union. Man himself is a union of both body and soul, and the separation that occurs at death is temporary, being healed and renewed at the general resurrection at the end of time.

There are between 150,000 and 400,000 Christian Scientists worldwide. The primary means of contact many outsiders have with the denomination is their popular newspaper, *The Christian Science Monitor*. Aside from local churches, many congregations may also maintain a Christian Science Reading Room, typically located in a downtown area.

JEHOVAH'S WITNESSES

The origins of the Jehovah's Witnesses lie in the 1870s in the preaching of Charles Taze Russell, whose group was originally called the Bible Student movement. Russell was a businessman from Pennsylvania involved in the Adventist movement in the nineteenth century. After becoming an agnostic in 1869, he later regained faith in God and began studying the Bible. His study led him to conclude, among other things, that Jesus had returned to the earth invisibly in 1874 in order to prepare for the Kingdom of God, which would be ushered in by Armageddon, set to take place in 1914.

All of these claims are similar to those of other Adventist groups, who had their own dates calculated for eschatological events. Russell's followers were expected to spend much of their time warning others about the imminent end of the world. Those who heeded the warnings would survive the coming first judgment, followed by a thousand-year reign of Christ on earth, followed by a second judgment. In the end, only 144,000 people from the whole of human history would actually make it to heaven.

Russell's original group suffered a number of schisms, and the majority of the members of the Bible Student movement dissociated themselves from the Watch Tower Society he founded. Those who remained came to form the main body of the modern denomination, which was organized along almost theocratic lines after the First World War by Joseph F. Rutherford, who predicted that Abraham, Isaac, Jacob, and the prophets would return to earth in 1925. In 1931 Rutherford renamed the group as the Jehovah's Witnesses, a reference to Isaiah 43:10.

Particularly during the period of Rutherford's leadership, the Witnesses often had an adversarial relationship with the American government, which led to a number of the laws enacted on the question of being a conscientious objector to avoid military service. In 1942, Rutherford died and was succeeded by Nathan Homer Knorr, who refocused the Witnesses away from cultural confrontation and toward missionary outreach. During Knorr's tenure, Armageddon was predicted to come in 1975, which was supposedly exactly six thousand years after the creation of Adam. Despite Knorr's predictions, Armageddon did not take place in 1975, and in 1977, Knorr died. His successor Frederick Franz explained that Armageddon would actually take place six thousand years after the creation of Eve, who was a few months or years younger than Adam. With Franz's death in 1993, the Witnesses were led by Milton Henschel, who resigned in 2000 and was followed by Don Adams.

The Jehovah's Witnesses emphasize their view of the biblical name of God, which in Hebrew is probably pronounced "Yahweh," but came to be Latinized over time into "Jehovah." The Witnesses say this is the true name of God. Mankind itself is a participant in a struggle for sovereignty between Jehovah and Satan. Jehovah himself does have a body, but it is a "spirit body."

Like the ancient Arian heretics, the Witnesses identify Jesus as a creation of God through whom the rest of creation was made. Jesus did perform miracles here on earth but does not perform them any more. He suffered and was killed, but it was not on a cross but rather a "torture stake," a single upright piece of wood. (The cross is regarded as a pagan symbol.) His death works to set human beings free from sin and death. After dying, he was resurrected by God as a "spirit creature." Jesus is also the same person as the Archangel Michael. The Holy Spirit is not a divine Person but rather is merely God's "active force."

The Witnesses use and believe in the Bible, though they have their own special translation called the *New World Translation*, which is an alteration of the biblical text to support their doctrines. John 1, for instance, instead of reading, "In the beginning was the Word, and the Word was with God, and the Word was God," reads, ". . . and the Word was *a god*." Their translation also inserts the word *Jehovah* into the New Testament 237 times without any correspondence to the original Greek text.

Hell does not exist for the Witnesses. It is simply a symbol for death. Instead, the wicked will be annihilated after Armageddon. Until that happens, all of the dead, both good and evil, are "conscious of nothing." (Note the similarity here to Adventist teaching on "soul sleep.") The beginning of the end did in fact occur in 1914, when Jehovah threw Satan and all the demons out of heaven, which is why world events have been getting progressively worse since then. The abolition of all world governments and the setting up of a theocracy ruled directly by God is predicted to come soon, though precise dates are no longer given.

After the end comes, 144,000 Jehovah's Witnesses will be given spirit bodies and live in heaven. The remainder of Jehovah's Witnesses will live in paradise on a restored earth. Everyone else will be annihilated, after being given a second chance to prove their obedience to God by becoming Jehovah's Witnesses. This arrangement into levels of salvation is similar to the ancient gnostic spiritual caste division of the truly "spiritual," the spiritual elite, and the merely "soulful," the average believer. Orthodoxy holds, however, that transfiguration by God and communion with Him are fully available to every human person. There is no spiritual caste system.

While Jehovah's Witnesses are not regarded as Christians by most Christian groups, they return the favor and regard themselves as the only Christians. Since they reject the use of the Cross, they often will use images of a watchtower, a reference not only to their earliest identity but also to the name of their publishing arm, the Watch Tower Bible and Tract Society. Their meeting places are not referred to as *churches* but rather as *Kingdom Halls*, a reference to their belief in the imminent establishment of God's Kingdom on Earth. Each Kingdom Hall, typically of simple, unadorned architecture, has no more than two hundred members, and members attend the Kingdom Hall closest to their home.

Jehovah's Witnesses are all strongly encouraged to engage in evangelistic activity, which is usually done by door-to-door visitation, typically with copies of their literature in hand (most often their two periodicals, *Awake!* and *The Watchtower*). Evangelism is often conducted by whole families visiting people's homes, offering to conduct free Bible studies. Everyone is expected to give monthly reports on their witnessing activities to the local congregation.

Witnesses also do not celebrate any religious holidays, with the exception of an annual observance of Christ's death, an event called the Memorial, which is dated by the Jewish calendar on the fourteenth of the month of Nisan (the traditional date for the Passover) and is open for anyone to attend. They reject Christmas and other Christian holidays, believing that all such acts are idolatry. They have no problem, however, with celebrations for weddings, birthdays, anniversaries, or funerals.

They refuse to salute the American flag, say the Pledge of Allegiance, or serve in the military, because doing so would constitute idolatry and treason against their true citizenship in God's Kingdom, which includes a literal government. The Witnesses also do not engage in any sort of inter-faith or inter-Christian activities or dialogue, because doing so would pollute the purity of their faith. They believe that blood transfusions are prohibited by the Bible, based on their reading of Acts 15:20, which Orthodoxy looks upon only as a prohibition against eating or drinking blood.

Witnesses baptize and hold communion, though both acts are regarded as purely symbolic. Their communion rite is held during the annual Memorial and uses unleavened bread and wine. Only those who claim to be among the 144,000 partake of the elements. Baptism is only for those "of a responsible age" and confers full membership.

Over the years, the Witnesses have changed a number of doctrines that formerly were regarded as essential. In addition, they believe that their organizational government is God's sole channel for communication with the world, often expressed in articles in the *Watchtower* magazine. Many articles in *The Watchtower* will warn against the dangers of independent thinking in an effort to keep Witnesses in line with the Watch Tower Society's teachings. The Society also strongly discourages members from exposing themselves to criticism of the Jehovah's Witnesses or to Bibles or other publications from outside the organization. Members are encouraged to shun former Jehovah's Witnesses, even family members, especially if they have been officially "disfellowshipped" for refusal to obey the leadership or for unrepentant sin.

All of this strongly contrasts with Orthodoxy, which places an emphasis on the free will of man and the possibility for every person to know God without fear that reading something is in itself harmful or threatening. In addition, while Orthodoxy will sometimes practice pastoral excommunication temporarily while a person is repenting, he is never to be systematically shunned, especially not by family members.

There are about seven million Jehovah's Witnesses in the world, and while their numbers are still growing, the rate of growth has slowed in recent years. They are particularly active among the black population in the United States.

UNIFICATION CHURCH ("MOONIES")

The Holy Spirit Association for the Unification of World Christianity, also known as the Unification Church, was founded by Sun Myung Moon in 1954. Its followers are commonly known as "Moonies," from the family name of their founder, though that term is often taken to be derogatory. In 1994, the official name of the church was changed to the Family Federation for World Peace and Unification.

Born in 1920 with the name Mun Yon-myung in what is now North Korea, Moon was raised in a family originally of Confucianist background, but converted with them to the Presbyterian Church in Korea at the age of ten.

Five years later, in 1935, according to official church accounts, Jesus appeared to Moon and asked him to complete the work left unfinished after the Crucifixion. After a period of prayer and consideration, he took up the task, changing his name to Mun Son-myung, which is usually rendered in Western sources as Sun Myung Moon (Korean names usually begin with the family name followed by the personal name, the reverse of the Western custom).

After lengthy study of the Bible, Moon began preaching his complex doctrines in 1946, leading to his excommunication by the Presbyterian Church. He eventually fled government persecution in 1950 and made his way into South Korea, where he founded the Unification Church in 1954. One of Moon's early converts, known as Miss Kim, had been prone in her early life to seeing visions, including at least one from Emanuel Swedenborg, and she was commissioned by Moon to become his first missionary to the United States. She moved to San Francisco and began the work there.

The Unification Church teaches that Moon is the Messiah, that he is the Second Coming of Jesus Christ. His teaching is termed the Divine Principle, which he claims to have received from God through divine inspiration, prayer, suffering, and the study of Scripture. The basic concept in the Divine Principle is that everything in nature comes in pairs, such as male and female, light and dark, positive and negative electrical charges, arteries and veins, and so forth. Understanding these pairs in the creation leads to knowledge of the Creator. From this, Moonies believe that God Himself is a duality of masculinity and femininity. Further, because human beings value love and harmony, we should conclude that "heart" is the inner essence of God. In addition to this inner essence, God has what is called the "universal prime energy," which sustains the universe. This idea is similar to the Orthodox teaching about God's divine energies, which are His actual presence in creation.

The purpose of all of creation is to enjoy love. Adam and Eve were created to attain to a "four position foundation" within "three blessings": (1) Becoming perfect, which is having God's character and being in the four positions, which here are God, the perfected individual, and the individual's mind and body. (2) Having an ideal marriage, in which the four positions consist of God, the husband, the wife, and their children. The offspring of such a marriage are perfect and sinless. (3) Having dominion over all creation, in which the four positions are God, man, things, and a dominion of love.

After the third blessing, the Kingdom of God would be established on earth. However, Adam and Eve fell short of their calling in two falls, a spiritual and a physical. The spiritual fall occurred when Eve had sexual relations with Lucifer. The physical fall occurred when, after Adam and Eve were ashamed, they consummated their marriage before they had completed the first blessing. Selfish love has subsequently dominated all human life.

In order for God's Kingdom to come to earth, someone has to become perfect, have an ideal marriage, and then propagate this perfection throughout all the earth until the Kingdom is established. Before these blessings can be fulfilled, however, two foundations have to be restored, the foundation of faith and the foundation of substance. John the Baptist is said to have restored the first to prepare the coming of the Messiah, by having perfect faith. The foundation of substance can only be restored if someone in the position of Lucifer humbles himself before someone in the position of Adam, because the foundation was originally broken by an angel (Lucifer), who reversed positions with mankind. This the Jews supposedly restored when they venerated John the Baptist, because they represented Cain while John represented Abel. This allowed Jesus to come into the world, but the foundations were subsequently destroyed again when John denied that he was Elijah and supposedly questioned Jesus' identity as the Messiah.

Jesus was able to restore the foundation of faith in His forty-day fast, but His people rejected Him and so He did not restore the foundation of substance. But Jesus allowed Satan to invade His spirit and was killed on the Cross. Three days later, His "spirit self" (but not His physical self) was resurrected, giving Him victory over Satan. When His disciples believed in Him, the foundation of substance was restored, making Him the Spiritual Messiah and providing salvation to believers. He did not, however, bring about physical salvation because He did not marry and have children, which is part of the completion of God's plan. This is where Sun Myung Moon comes in.

The Unification Church teaches that for four hundred years before the coming of Moon, God was preparing the world through events such as the Protestant Reformation and the Great Awakenings in the United States and Great Britain. From calculations based on the Bible, it was determined that the Second Messiah (or the Second Coming) would have to be born in Korea between 1918 and 1930. Moon's coming was to complete the work of Jesus, and the children that he and his wife have conceived are the first in human history since Adam and Eve to be born without original sin. Moon and his wife are "co-messiahs" who are the "True Parents" of all mankind, God incarnate on earth in both His feminine and masculine aspects. Other members of the "True Family" are highly regarded, and at least two of them have had officially sanctioned mediums channeling them after death.

Moon's followers get married and imitate him. Their children are thus also born without original sin. In this way, through marriage and propagation, the Unification Church is establishing the Kingdom of God on earth. The Moonies are therefore very much against premarital sex, infidelity, divorce, and homosexuality, as all are distortions of the perfect pairing of husband and wife. The Moonies are perhaps best known for their mass wedding ceremonies, which often include marriages arranged by the Unification Church. The ceremony itself is complicated and believed to wipe away the sins of the couple, which then permits them to have sinless children. Interestingly, Moonie honeymoons consist of forty days of sexual abstinence.

Besides the creation of perfect families, the Unification Church teaches that there are three "indemnity conditions" that have to be fulfilled in order for the three blessings to come. The first and second were satisfied by the First and Second World Wars. World War III, which is imminent, will satisfy the third. After this happens, all humanity will be united together with God in a four position foundation, and the world will enjoy eternal peace, joy, and love.

Orthodox Christianity is completely different in most respects from the teachings of the Unification Church. We share some of the same concepts and some of the same historical events, but our understanding of those concepts, people, and events is quite different. Most of all, we do not believe that Sun Myung Moon is the Messiah, nor do we believe in the complex array of cosmological foundations and blessings the Moonies teach about.

Salvation for the Orthodox can exist with or without marriage, and marriage itself is solely for the purpose of the salvation of the husband, wife, and children. Though we do not believe in the Western concept of original sin, we do believe that all mankind is born with ancestral mortality, which introduced corruption into the human person, bringing with it the tendency to sin. Everyone is born with this, no matter how holy their parents are. The basic problem with the teachings of the Unification Church, aside from their being radically divorced from the Holy Tradition of Orthodox Christianity, is one of history. History is reinterpreted in bizarre ways, more reminiscent of the vast cosmological speculations of the gnostics than of the concrete history of salvation as described in the Bible.

The Moonies have a presence in roughly a hundred countries. They claim a membership of about 3 million, but other sources put their numbers at between 250,000 and 1 million.

CONCLUSIONS

The origins of these various non-mainstream religious bodies yield another demonstration of what happens when the notion takes hold that the individual person is the arbiter of what is true, especially when one accepts that true Christianity has been lost at some point in history. If a Lutheran can stand up and say that Joseph Smith is not to be believed, then one has to wonder why Martin Luther should be believed. While both represent major disjunctions from traditional Christianity, both also claimed to be restoring ancient and true Christianity.

The religions we have just described are generally rejected by mainstream denominationalist Protestant Christianity. Yet, if Swedenborg is wrong, then why is Calvin right? If Mary Baker Eddy is wrong, then why is John Wesley right? If Sun Myung Moon is wrong, then why is Billy Graham right? All of these people claimed an authority divorced from the Church and then founded or motivated vast religious movements based on their personal authority. The only conclusion we can draw is that critics of these various groups simply think they are too weird or too different from what they themselves believe. Once again, the individual believer is made to be the arbiter of all truth.

At least one lesson we learn from this chapter is that everyone draws the line somewhere. How it is that mainstream denominationalism can disagree over things like whether baptism does anything for you or whether your salvation is predetermined before all time by God without your input, and yet all call each other "Christian," seems to me, at least, to be a bit arbitrary. It reflects a minimalist understanding of theology—that only certain issues are truly essential, while most are of secondary importance. While the Orthodox agree that there are essential questions and less essential ones, our understanding of the essentials of the Christian faith is not minimalist but rather maximalist—the Orthodox Christian faith is a whole life, not a minimum set of doctrines. Further, that life is to be lived within the one Church established by Christ, not between any number of denominations who all disagree on major issues and yet somehow still recognize each other's legitimacy.

In a real sense, the Mormons, Jehovah's Witnesses, and so on all represent a sort of "outer rim" of Protestantism. All claim to be Christian. All claim to have a true interpretation of the Bible. All were founded by people with a background in mainstream Protestant denominations. These non-mainstream groups simply represent another set of schisms from Protestantism. Certainly, most Protestants would not even recognize these people as Christian, but they share a common founding principle: If someone has a different interpretation of the Bible or of what Christianity should be, he can found his own church.

This approach contrasts with Orthodoxy, which teaches that the Son of God came to earth at a moment in history, was born of the Virgin Mary, lived, died, and rose from the dead, founding His one Church through the Apostles. All departures from this clear Gospel message, as we have seen, lead to quite dangerous spiritual results.

Seven

Non-Christian Religions

MANY PATHS, MANY DESTINATIONS

One of the most common assertions made by those who describe themselves as "spiritual but not religious" is that all religions are really trying to accomplish the same thing—that all of them are legitimate paths to God. Such an assertion is typically influenced, however, by the context of pluralistic American society, which is most often defined by various forms of Christianity. These different Christian groups may use the same terminology and the same rituals and share many doctrines, but as we have seen, they are very much not the same. Yet to a casual observer, it may appear that they are all working toward the same goal, salvation in Jesus Christ, but that some minor details are at issue. This viewpoint, however, is only possible to hold under the influence of Pietism.

If the various Christian groups are fundamentally headed in different directions, even a cursory examination of the rest of the world's religions will reveal even more widely diverging paths. To assert that all religions are really just different paths to God is a denial of the central tenets of these religions. The Hindu Yogin trying to achieve oblivion and utter absorption into the faceless universe is not on the same path as the Jew bowing down before the God of Abraham, Isaac, and Jacob, or the Scientologist working to become "clear" of alien beings called "thetans." To suggest that all these believers are really on the same path is to do damage to their theological systems—to assert that somehow we know better than these people do what their teachings really are. Yet it is a fundamental rule of any religious study that one should let believers speak for themselves as to what they believe and, most especially, what they are trying to achieve in their religion.

A somewhat more sophisticated approach to this question is called Perennialism, and it asserts that there is an esoteric core to be found at the heart of the orthodox versions of all major world religions. This esoteric core is supposedly the same in every faith, and so every faithful follower of an orthodox religion is validly on his way to divine enlightenment. Yet the Perennialist must decide for himself what constitutes this esoteric core and what does not, despite what the leaders and sacred texts of those religions may say about themselves. He has to say that he knows what the real truth inside a religion is, better than does its entire tradition regarding itself. Again, this is a violation of the basic integrity of these religions. Who is the Perennialist to say what is truly at the heart of a faith and what is not?

That being said, as we mentioned at the beginning of this book, the Orthodox Church has always believed that there is a seed of the truth, Jesus Christ Himself, in every religion and philosophy. That seed is often obscured by error, but it is nevertheless there. The ancient pagan Egyptians, for instance, believed that Pharaoh was an incarnate god—the intuition is correct, even if the identification is not. This theme of the seed of truth is to be found in the second-century Christian writer St. Justin Martyr, who himself had been an ardent follower of several pagan philosophical schools before he became an Orthodox Christian. He saw in them what he called the *spermatikos Logos*, the "Word in seed form." Thus, even while we look critically at other religious traditions, we also must see in them the possibility for their believers to cultivate the truth they have and, with that, come to the fullness of the truth in Jesus Christ, as revealed in His Church.

St. Justin's view, which is the Orthodox view, contrasts with the Perennialist's in that he is looking for Jesus Christ in all other belief systems. He has not distilled out a supposed esoteric core from all major religions and then discarded the rest as inessential to those religions. He also regards Orthodox Christianity as the fullness of the revelation of God to mankind, maintaining that only in the Church can man encounter that revelation in its wholeness. For the Perennialist, there would be no point in conversion from one religion to another, but for the Orthodox Church, all of mankind is invited into communion with God in the Church.

In this chapter, we will briefly examine most of the world's major non-Christian religions, as well as a few minor ones that Americans may encounter. Unfortunately, our examination of all these groups will necessarily be highly simplified and generalized, due to space constraints. Whole books and even series of books have been written on these subjects, so we cannot pretend to do them full justice in one chapter. Although I have studied all of them to one extent or another, I am by no means an expert on any of these religions. What we are attempting to present here is an encyclopedia-level view, a brief summary of the major points.

We can make at least two generalizations about all of these faiths. None of them believes in the Holy Trinity, the Father, Son, and Holy Spirit, three divine Persons who are One in essence. None of them believes that Jesus Christ is the Son of God, the second Person of the Holy Trinity, who became incarnate to save mankind, died and rose from the dead, and ascended into heaven.

JUDAISM

Of all non-Christian religions, the one with which Orthodox Christians have the most in common is Judaism. We might be tempted to look at Judaism and say, "We came from you!" In some sense, this is correct, but we must understand some history in order to comprehend what the true relationship is. Historically and sociologically, Orthodox Christianity is not the child of what is now Orthodox Judaism, but rather its older brother. How can this be?

Judaism as we see it in our own time is not the religion of Abraham, Isaac, Jacob, and Moses. That faith died theologically at the Day of Pentecost in AD 33, when the Church came into her fullness and became the New Israel. That faith died sociologically and historically in the year AD 70, when the Temple in Jerusalem was destroyed by the Romans. In some Jewish traditions, it is said that the *shekhinah* (the divine glory and presence of God) deserted the Temple when it was destroyed. (The *shekhinah* plays a significant part in Kabbalah, a mystical offshoot of Rabbinic Judaism.)

The Temple was the center of the religion of Moses, the center of the Jewish priesthood and its sacrificial cult. All Jews went to the Temple every so often to make sacrifices, especially on high holy days such as the Passover. But when the Temple was destroyed, the priestly line was ended. No more sacrifices could be made. What was left were the synagogues, provisional places of teaching and learning—but not sacrifice—which served as local branches of the Jewish faith.

Judaism in the time of Christ encompassed multiple sects and movements (e.g., the Pharisees, Sadducees, Essenes, Herodians, and Zealots), all with different sets of beliefs but a generally common set of practices. With the destruction of the Temple, these groups mostly disappeared, with the exception of one, the Pharisees. It was the sect of the Pharisees that survived, and so they came to define Judaism and practice it based on a new pattern of life that did not include the Temple sacrifices. Thus was born Judaism as it exists today.

Pharisaism, as shown in the New Testament, had always focused more on a set of practices rather than a set of beliefs, and so even though there were and remain definite beliefs that go along with Judaism, what is most important is a way of life, following particular rituals and perhaps most famously, dietary requirements. Orthodox Christianity shares this emphasis with Judaism on adopting a whole way of life designed to bring the remembrance of God into every moment, and some of our practices are even based on our common ancestor of Temple Judaism. But the Orthodox Church also places a high emphasis on right belief, which is what informs and shapes our way of life. Christianity cannot be reduced to an ethical or ritual system, which is a temptation for Judaism.

Jews reject major Christian doctrine, such as the Holy Trinity, the Incarnation of Jesus Christ, and His identification as the Messiah. Jews are still awaiting the coming of the Messiah. We do share with Jews a belief in monotheism, that there is only one God. While we do not share the same Bible (Jews have only a portion of our Old Testament), we do share a common outlook on biblical interpretation, namely, that there is both a "written Torah" and an "oral Torah"—two sources of true religious tradition, each of which informs and shapes the other. (*Torah* is the Jewish name for the first five books of the Bible, but also for the Law of Moses in general.) We also share a common belief in divine revelation from God through the Prophets, though we believe that the Prophets ultimately were predicting the coming of Jesus and that God made His final revelation to the Apostles at Pentecost.

Jews may believe in an afterlife. Ancient Pharisaism believed in the final resurrection of the dead, something that it shares with Orthodox Christianity. (St. Paul famously shows his Pharisaic credentials in terms of his belief in the resurrection in Acts 23:6.) Jews believe they are God's chosen people, a status primarily conferred by maternal ancestry, though conversion is possible. Orthodox Christianity regards the Church as God's chosen people, and all membership is through conversion. (Even a baby who is baptized is not born an Orthodox Christian.) The Orthodox Church regards itself as the New Israel; the theological status of Israel was forfeited by the Jews when they rejected Jesus. Jews of today regard themselves as the children of Abraham and followers of Moses, despite their religion having been sundered from the sacrificial cult in the Temple.

Modern Judaism is split into three general groups—Orthodox, Conservative, and Reform. In general, these groups represent a continuum from traditionalism to liberalism. In the modern state of Israel, only Orthodox Jews are legally regarded as Jews. Depending on how identity as a Jew is defined, there may be as many as 15 million Jews in the world.

ISLAM

Islam's traditional account of itself is that Muhammad, who is claimed to be the last of the Prophets, received a word-for-word dictation from the Archangel Gabriel, which is now known as the Qur'an. This revelation supposedly took place in the year AD 622.

Islam regards its relationship to Christianity in a manner similar to the way Christians regard ancient Judaism: that it is the final fulfillment of previous Abrahamic religion. Islam sees Jesus as a true prophet and believes in His virgin conception and birth, as well as His second coming. Islam is radically monotheistic, however, and rejects the doctrine of the Trinity and even the idea that God (in Arabic, *Allah*) could have a son. Trinitarianism is looked upon by Muslims as disguised polytheism. Muslims also frown upon icons, saying that neither God nor any other living thing should be depicted (which is why traditional Muslim art has a highly developed calligraphy but not a tradition of pictorial representation).

Muslims regard the Christian Bible as having been corrupted over time, believing that the original teachings of Jesus were essentially Muslim. The Qur'an, by contrast, is supposedly a direct dictation from God Himself in Arabic. This belief runs into serious problems, however, when variant manuscripts of the Qur'an are unearthed. If it is true that the Qur'an was dictated by an angel, how does one explain contradictory manuscript traditions? A Muslim asking such questions publicly may find himself persecuted.

Muslims believe that proper life consists in adhering to the five pillars of Islam: (1) *Shahadah*—The confession, "I testify that there is none worthy of worship except God and I testify that Muhammad is the Messenger of God." Making this confession with sincerity is what converts someone to Islam. (2) *Salah*—Ritual prayer performed five times a day, facing toward Mecca. (3) *Zakat*—Almsgiving, both to help the poor and for the spread of Islam. (4) *Sawm*—Fasting during the month of Ramadan, which consists of not eating anything at all before sunset. In practice, however, many Muslims will simply sleep through the day and then feast at night. (5) *Hajj*—A one-time pilgrimage to Mecca for all those who can afford it.

Orthodox Christians share all of these elements of proper life in various ways, although they are not regarded as absolute obligations as they are for Muslims. The very word *Islam* means "submission," and so obedience is key to the character of Muslim life. For Orthodoxy, the obedience we offer to God is given freely out of love for Him, and because doing so transforms us inwardly to become more like Christ. In Islam, God is merciful and perfect, but He is not truly loving. God is absolutely transcendent, and so there is no true communion with Him. Perhaps the only exception to this is the Sufi tradition of Islam, which has a strong mystical side.

In a real sense, Islam has a truly pagan side—a strongly tribal tendency; a relationship with God based on obedience, reward, and punishment; and most especially the fatalistic pursuit of self-sacrifice for the sake of the tribe or nation. This sociological character contrasts with the multicultural universalism of Christianity, the relationship of love between God and man, and the sacrifice of Jesus on the cross and His resurrection for the salvation of mankind. Our understanding of God and our relationship with Him is deeply different from that of Muslims. Given this, there are some Christians who identify Allah as a different "god" entirely, but *Allah* is in fact simply the Arabic word for "God," used by Arabic-speaking Christians as well. Islam is simply wrong about who Allah is.

Islam is itself divided, with the most major divisions being Sunni and Shi'a. These two groups share much in common, though with different doctrinal emphases and contrasting views on who was the proper heir of Muhammad as caliph (essentially a theocratic leader) in the first years after Muhammad's death. Each group regards the other as heretical and itself as the true Islam. All Islam shares the general belief in the absolute union of religion and the state. Theocracy is the Muslim ideal.

There is of course a great deal of debate going on in our time as to whether Islam is inherently violent, whether the *jihad* ("struggle") expected of all Muslims is only an interior spiritual struggle or a call to war against non-Muslims. We can say with certainty, however, that many historical Muslims saw it precisely as a call to war, which is one of the major reasons the Middle East, what is now Turkey, and much of western Asia are all now majority Muslim areas and not Orthodox Christian as they formerly were. All of those regions were conquered in the name of Allah by the sword. There have been a great many martyrs for the Orthodox faith under Islam.

Islam is the second largest religious group in the world, with over one billion members. About 85 to 90 percent are Sunni Muslims, while the remaining are Shi'a. The Sufi are particular mystical groups within both Sunni and Shi'a Islam. (*Dervish* is a Turkish term for a Sufi, derived from Persian.)

DRUZE

The Druze, whose origins lie in early eleventh-century Egypt, are in some ways an offshoot of Shi'a Islam, but their faith incorporates elements of Hellenistic neoplatonism and gnosticism. Their founder was the Persian mystic Hamza ibn-'Ali ibn-Ahmad, who gathered a large group of Muslim scholars and teachers together in Egypt and formed his movement. Although their beliefs differ from mainstream Islam, they are often considered to be Muslims by other Muslims, most often because Druze are usually quite secretive about their faith. They may often deliberately identify themselves as Muslims in order to avoid persecution.

The Druze concept of God is almost pantheistic—that God is not "above" everything or "in" everything, but rather that He is "the whole of existence." In any event, the emphasis is on the oneness and the unlimited nature of God. Despite the insistence on His unlimited nature, God is still understood as being "other" than the creation. Ultimately, this teaching about God is not completely incompatible with Orthodoxy, though we would not say that God is "the whole of existence," but rather that He is both "above" and "in" everything, that His being "other" than what is created by no means limits Him.

Individual Druze mystics who are spiritually advanced claim to experience God as a light that may be manifest in them. This light is not to be understood as an incarnation as in Christianity, but rather almost in the sense that we understand saints—that God is apparent within them, without the saint becoming fused with God. This kind of enlightenment is only available to a rare few. Druze are strongly esoteric in their theology and have at least three levels of teaching which are revealed to believers only at certain stages. Most believers will never receive all the teachings of the faith, and about 80 percent are officially defined as a sort of "non-religious class" who mainly practice personal prayer without the more esoteric teachings of the faith. In this, the Druze are like the ancient gnostics, who believed in secret teachings only available to a special few. The Christian Gospel, by contrast, is preached openly to all who will listen.

There are between 750,000 and 2 million Druze in the world. The largest communities are in Syria, with significant communities also existing in Lebanon, Israel, and Jordan, as well as in immigrant communities outside the Middle East.

ZOROASTRIANISM

Zoroastrianism was once the dominant religion of what was the Persian Empire, centered in modern Iran. Its origins date to roughly one thousand years before the birth of Jesus Christ. The founder of the religion is Zoroaster (or Zarathustra), who claimed to be a prophet from Ahura Mazda, the one, true god.

Zoroastrians share with Orthodox Christians a belief in one, uncreated God, to whom all worship is due. Zoroastrian goodness, however, is not understood, as in Christianity, as love and communion with God, but rather as order. Thus, evil is chaos. In the Orthodox Church, however, while we believe that God is a God of order, we do not identify goodness with order in itself. Rather, goodness is an aspect of God's character.

In Zoroastrianism, those who actively participate in all areas of life, including pleasure, with good thoughts, words, and deeds will have happiness. Active participation is key, and contemplative ways of life, such as monasticism, are rejected. This contrasts with Orthodoxy, which teaches that suffering in this life will often come to the righteous, and that only in the next life will the triumph of good finally be revealed. Orthodoxy also embraces asceticism, a focusing of the human person on what is good, even to the extent of denying oneself what is morally neutral so as to better practice good.

For Zoroastrians, there are in some sense angels and demons, though rather than being separate persons, they are "divine sparks" emanated by the one god, Ahura Mazda, personifications of aspects of his creation.

At the end of time, a savior figure (a *Saoshyant*) will appear and drive all evil from the world. Even the souls previously banished to "darkness" will be recalled, and all the dead will be resurrected. Those who died in old age will be made alive in immortal "spiritual" bodies about forty years of age, while those who died young will be about fifteen years of age. These bodies will be so insubstantial that they will not cast shadows. In the end, everyone will enjoy this restoration, and all humanity will be united in one nation speaking one language. This eschatology has certain similarities to Orthodoxy, but we have no speculations as to what "age" anyone will be in the afterlife. We also believe that in the Resurrection, we will all have bodies that can be touched and are substantial, just as Jesus' was after His Resurrection.

Zoroastrian worship strongly centers on the fire cult. In this cult, which is served by priests, fire is highly revered and is believed to mediate the spirit of Ahura Mazda to worshipers. Zoroastrians would not say that they worship fire, but rather that the fire serves as a connecting point to Ahura Mazda. Such ritual fires are so highly prized that ashes from particular sacred fires are brought to new places to act as a seed for a new fire temple. It is believed that some of these successions of ashes go back to Zoroaster himself. The ashes are also used for anointing, such as in the initiation ritual that makes one a member of the faith.

There are no Zoroastrian missionaries in our own time. Although it is possible to convert to the faith, most Zoroastrians keep to themselves and do not actively encourage conversion. Orthodoxy, by contrast, has missionary outreach as a central tenet of living the faith.

Today, there are only about 90,000 Zoroastrians left in the world, 75 percent of whom live in India and are called Parsees. Most of the rest live in their traditional homeland of Iran, with a few in Pakistan. Zoroastrianism's dominance in the region came to an end with the Muslim invasions of the seventh century.

MANDAEISM

Mandaeism is a monotheistic faith whose traditional homeland is in modern Iraq (though many Mandaeans fled Iraq after the 2003 American invasion). The earliest written accounts of these people date to the late eighth century. They have a great reverence for many figures from the Jewish Old Testament, such as Adam, Abel, and Noah, and they especially venerate John the Baptist. They may also be called Sabians.

There are no basic written guides to Mandaean theology, which exists primarily as a set of traditions held in common by believers. Like most monotheists, Mandaeans believe in a supreme spiritual entity, though this deity delegates the act of creation to lesser beings. Our own universe was created by the Archetypal Man, who created our world in his own image. (Note the similarity though not identity with the Christian doctrine that creation comes through the Son of God.)

Reality is largely characterized by the dualism of gnostic theology, with spirit opposed to matter, as well as other cosmic pairings, such as a cosmic Father and Mother, left and right, light and dark. As in Platonism, a world of ideas exists that has a stronger reality than the world of physical matter. The human soul is therefore a captive in this physical world, and the supreme entity is the soul's true home to which it will eventually return.

Mandaeans have their own astrology, believing that planets and stars influence human life. These celestial bodies are places of the detention of souls after death. Worlds of light may be reached after death with the assistance of savior spirits. The soul may also be purified in this life through the aid of ritual mysteries with a highly symbolic and esoteric interpretation attached to them, including baptism (*musbattah*). Such rituals are only fully explained to initiates, who pledge themselves to secrecy with this knowledge.

These rituals are usually practiced in a *manda*, which, due to the central place of water in Mandaean life, is traditionally built beside a river, but may also include a bath inside a building. The ritual life of Mandaeism is governed by a priesthood, who are sharply distinguished from the laity and are regarded as superior beings.

Mandaean scripture is a large corpus of varied writings that have never been codified into a systematic theology. The traditions in them focus largely on a discrete division between light and darkness, with light being associated with the supreme entity and darkness with Ptahil, who is the corrupted, archetypal man who created our world. (Ptahil's name is clearly similar to the pagan Egyptian deity Ptah, who called the world into being. Mandaean tradition includes accounts of their presence in Egypt.) The earliest texts in Mandaean scripture date to the second and third centuries.

While venerating as prophets Adam, his son Abel, and grandson Enosh, as well as Noah and his son Shem and grandson Aram, Mandaeans regard Abraham and Moses as false prophets. (Noah and his descendants are supposedly the Mandaeans' ancestors.) Jerusalem itself is a city of wickedness, dedicated to the false god of the Jews, Adunay (from Hebrew *Adonai*, "the Lord"). They also regard Jesus and Muhammad as false prophets. Jesus in particular is accused of having corrupted the teachings entrusted to Him by John the Baptist, who is the highest and most respected teacher in Mandaeism.

For the Orthodox, Mandaeism is a gnostic-style religion that gets certain things right, such as monotheism, but is wildly distorted on other issues, such as the overall narrative of salvation in God's plan for the world. Probably the most major problem with Mandaeism is its cosmology, the idea that the physical world is the creation of a corrupt entity and not the work of the loving God.

It is possible that Mani, the founder of Manichaeism (a heretical sect from which St. Augustine converted when he became Christian), may have been a member of a sect called the Elkasaites, whom some scholars have proposed as the ancestors of the Mandaeans. There are only about 70,000 Mandaeans in the world, and while most of them lived in Iraq until 2003, a number of them have fled into Iran and other neighboring countries. As of 2009, there were perhaps only as many as twenty-four Mandaeans in the priesthood.

YAZIDISM

The Yazidi are monotheists following an ancient religion with roots in Indo-Iranian culture, primarily in Kurdish communities near the Turkish-Iraqi border. Along with the Alevi and Yarsan, the Yazidi are classified into a general grouping known as Yazdanism, which altogether makes up about one third of the Kurdish population (most Kurds are Sunni Muslims).

Yazidism is a syncretistic faith with elements of Sufi Islam, Christianity, Mithraism (a pagan cult originating in Persia), and other pre-Muslim pagan traditions of the Mesopotamian region. Its foundations as a distinct community are traced to the twelfth-century sheikh Adi ibn Musafir al-Umawi (also called Shex Adi), whom the Yazidi regard as being an avatar or reincarnation of Melek Taus (or Tawuse Melek), the Peacock Angel.

Sheikh Adi was a Sufi of Umayyad descent born in the Beqaa Valley of Lebanon who spent much of his early life in Baghdad and eventually took up residence in the Kurdish regions of Iraq to live a life of asceticism. While there, he impressed many of the locals with miraculous accomplishments. His tomb is in Lalish, northeast of Mosul, and is the principal shrine for Yazidi pilgrimage, where all Yazidi are expected to visit at least once in their lives.

Yazidi believe that God is the creator of the world and that He has placed the care of the world into the hands of the Heptad, seven angels through whom He created Adam. The world was created initially as a pearl and then later reconstructed and expanded to its current state. The chief of the seven angels is Melek Taus, who is also called *Shaytan* ("Satan"), leading Muslims and Christians in the area to identify the Yazidi as devil-worshipers. The Yazidi do not regard Melek Taus as evil, however, but as the leader of the angels, which is of course similar to the Christian understanding of Lucifer in his pre-fallen state. Evil is believed to find its source only in the human heart.

When Adam was created, Melek Taus is supposed to have been given the choice by God to bow down to him or not. He chose not to bow down, which was in keeping with the nature God had given him, that he should never bow to anyone. From this primordial choice of good over evil, Yazidi derive inspiration for their own choices for good over evil, and devotion to Melek Taus helps believers to make the right choices. Curiously, the Yazidi regard themselves as descended solely from Adam, while all other humans are descended from both Adam and Eve.

The seven angelic beings are believed to be reincarnated in human form (*koasasa*) every so often. It may also be possible for lesser Yazidi souls to be reincarnated in a process called *kiras guhorin* ("changing the garment"). During the annual festival of *Cejna Cemaiya* ("Feast of the Assembly") at Lalish, it is believed that the Heptad descend on Lalish. During this festival, a bull is also sacrificed at the shrine of Sheikh Adi.

The Yazidi do have their own scriptures, the *Kiteba Cilwe* ("Book of Revelation") and *Mishefa Resh* ("Black Book"), but the available manuscripts for these books, published in 1911 and 1913, are regarded by scholars as probable forgeries, though their contents are consistent with Yazidi tradition. There may once have been authentic copies of these texts, but they remain obscure. Yazidism is mainly transmitted through oral tradition, which in our day is beginning to be written down.

Like Muslims, Yazidi practice five prayers each day. They also maintain a strict system of religious purity, including a caste system of three levels in which members only marry within their caste. Purity is also maintained by not violating the four elements of earth, air, fire, and water (it is forbidden, for instance, to spit on water, fire, or earth). Likewise, Yazidi avoid contact with non-Yazidi, which can be spiritually polluting as well. They also will not wear the color blue (possibly because it usurps the color of the Peacock Angel). Children are baptized at birth, and boys are frequently circumcised. Conversion to Yazidism is not possible, because Yazidis may only be those who are descended solely from Adam.

Orthodox Christians can admire the Yazidi desire for personal purity, though much of its actual expression is based on pagan superstitions rather than the revelation of God in Christ. As with all syncretistic religious systems, there are parts that are familiar and acceptable to Christians, but there are also elements we must reject. Christians do not believe in castes, nor do they worship angels. Likewise, we do not believe in reincarnation, nor do we sacrifice animals.

Estimates of Yazidi population range from 500,000 to 700,000, mostly in Iraq.

BAHA'I FAITH

The Baha'i faith is a monotheistic religion founded in nineteenth-century Persia by Baha'u'llah, who claimed to be a fulfillment of Babism, a mid-nineteenth-century Messianic Muslim community that broke from Shi'a Islam. The faith's single most identifying feature is religious universalism—the teaching that all major religions in the world were founded by true prophets, who each progressively revealed something about God to the world and predicted the coming of the next prophet. The universe itself is regarded as being eternal.

Each of these prophets is regarded as a "manifestation of God," not an incarnation, but rather a semi-divine intermediary between God and man that existed spiritually before his birth as a human. With the coming of the Baha'i faith, however, all previous religions are revealed as being one single religion with a progressive revelation to mankind. Unlike Jesus or Muhammad, Baha'u'llah did not claim to be the last of these manifestations, and so there may yet be more revelations to come. Orthodoxy teaches that the final revelation of God to man came in Jesus Christ. We don't have to worry about whether the true religion will suddenly change underneath us with the appearance of a new prophet.

Because the Baha'i faith believes that it is the fulfillment of all other world religions, it reinterprets previous religious doctrine in its own terms. Trinitarian theology, for instance, rather than revealing the nature of God, is understood symbolically to refer to different aspects of God (essentially a form of Sabellianism). Thus, even though Baha'is claim to accept all religious teachings within themselves, they must fundamentally change those doctrines in order to harmonize them according to Baha'i teaching. A believer in one of these other faiths cannot help but conclude that Baha'is (like Perennialists) are claiming to know other faiths better than their followers themselves do.

The Baha'i faith emphasizes acceptance of all religions and all people, and so it can be highly attractive in our modern, relativistic age. Yet underneath, the Baha'i faith is revealed simply as another new set of dogmas that revises old dogmas according to its own purposes. Many who convert to the Baha'i faith may do so because they believe it to be an embrace of true equality and freedom from dogma and tradition. The faith even teaches that all humanity should learn a single language to further perfect oneness.

Orthodox Christianity teaches, however, that all of us are truly of equal value in Christ and may commune with Him. This communion is only fully possible within the dogmatic and traditional boundaries of the Church, however, not because those boundaries limit human life but because they free human beings to become who they were created to be. Dogma and tradition are thus like the universal knowledge among athletes of what it takes to become truly fit.

Because the Baha'i faith has no doctrine of the Incarnation, while the believer may grow closer and closer to God, there is no sense of true communion with Him. The closest the Baha'i can ever get is "standing in the presence of God," which nevertheless implies a certain distance from Him. Orthodoxy teaches that in baptism, we put on Christ and He takes up residence in us. We are gradually more and more united with Him and partake of the very life of the Holy Trinity more fully, following a potentially infinite progression.

Population estimates of Baha'is are around 5 to 6 million, and the religion has seen some success among middle-class suburbanites in America.

HINDUISM

There really is no such thing as Hinduism. Essentially, *Hinduism* is a group label for a collection of religions and associated traditions that range from classically pagan—a single tribe worshiping its individual god or gods—to a kind of monotheism. Some Hindus believe in multiple gods. Others believe there is only one God, and everything is part of Him. Still others believe there is one God who may occasionally manifest Himself in various forms, avatars which have been mistaken by certain tribes as separate gods. Therefore, it is extremely difficult to define Hinduism. The word *Hindu* itself does not refer to any religion but rather to the region of the Indus River valley. In English, however, *Hindu* has come to refer to the religious traditions of that area.

Despite the great variation in Hindu beliefs and practices, there are certain common sets of belief which most Hindus share, whose origins stretch into roughly 1700–1100 BC. These beliefs are interpreted differently depending on one's tradition or the teachings of a guru.

For most Hindus, the human soul (the *atman*) is eternal. For some, the soul is a part of Brahman ("God," the universe), and so salvation consists in realizing this fact and being absorbed back into the oblivion of non-personality. For others, the one God or the gods have a personal existence and may be worshiped.

Most Hindus believe in *karma*, a sort of universal justice in which those who do good are rewarded, while those who do evil are punished. This justice is not necessarily the act of a god, but is rather in some sense the laws of nature. Most Hindus seek to gain good karma, perhaps through good deeds or devotion to a god, so that they may experience a better life here and now or in their next incarnation. The traditional purpose of the ascetical practices of yoga, however, is to rid oneself of all karma, whether good or bad, so that one can escape the cycle of reincarnation entirely. Thus, not all Hindus have the same religious goals.

Because the soul is immortal, it may be reincarnated into a new life, whether as a human being or as an animal. Reincarnation is influenced by one's karma, and so a truly good person may become reincarnated as a member of a higher caste in the next life. Likewise, an evil person may be reborn into a lower caste or even as an animal.

Most Hindu traditions have no problem with logical paradox, which is a similarity with Orthodoxy. Nonetheless, perhaps the hardest part in talking about Christ to Hindus is in showing Him to be the one, true God. Many Hindus will gladly accept Christ as yet another god or as an avatar of Brahman, because that is consistent with their religious system. The greatest difference between Hinduism and Orthodox Christianity is Orthodoxy's particularism—the teaching that there is one God, who revealed Himself as one man, the God-man, who founded one Church, which shares one Lord, one faith, one baptism.

Hinduism has become popular in the United States since the early 1970s, although usually in less traditional, more watered-down forms palatable to Americans. Hindus collectively make up the world's third largest religious grouping, with about one billion adherents.

BUDDHISM

Buddhism is an offshoot of Hinduism, essentially a sort of philosophized version of the basic Hindu teachings. It originated at least four hundred years before the birth of Christ with the teachings of Siddhartha Gautama, most commonly known as the Buddha (the "Awakened One"). In its essence, Buddhism is atheistic, believing in no god at all. It is therefore sometimes said to be a philosophy rather than a religion. Nonetheless, some Buddhists will worship Buddha himself as a sort of god.

Like Hinduism, Buddhism also believes in karma, as well as the cycle of reincarnation. This cycle is called *samsara*, the endless experience of suffering.

All of life, according to Buddhism, is suffering, and so escape from life and the cycle of rebirth is the highest goal. This escape is referred to as *nirvana*. Following the path of the Buddha is the only way to achieve nirvana. Those who achieve it are dispassionate, not pulled in any direction by desire. Nirvana is possible in this life, and after death, one who has achieved it is not bound by time or *samsara* any longer. He has been absorbed into non-distinction, his distinct personality obliterated.

Buddhists traditionally believe that every man's path is his own, and so they do not send missionaries, nor are they usually involved in any sort of charitable work. Buddhism is highly individualistic and most traditionally and fully expressed in Buddhist monasticism, where the Buddhist is free to pursue nirvana on his own. All Buddhists try to live in total moderation, neither descending into pleasure nor rejecting it entirely. There are various schools of Buddhism, which differ somewhat in their teachings as to how to achieve nirvana. Perhaps the most well-known of these schools in the West is Zen Buddhism, which emphasizes experience over the study of religious texts.

Orthodoxy shares certain things with Buddhism that are largely absent from Western Christianity, such as the emphasis on universal asceticism and dispassion. However, the purpose of Orthodox asceticism is not to be released from this world, but rather to bring the body under the soul's rule and thus enable a life fully in Christ. Further, Orthodox dispassion is not apathetic toward the suffering of others but is deeply compassionate. Finally, salvation in Orthodoxy is not the attainment of non-self, but rather the full realization of self in communion with God.

Buddhism has two major branches, Theraveda and Mahayana. There are about 350 million Buddhists in the world, centered in Tibet, China, Japan, Korea, and Southeast Asia.

JAINISM

Perhaps the most religiously pacifistic people in the world are the Jains of eastern India, who number more than four million believers. Jainism is similar to Hinduism in its belief in reincarnation and the transmigration of souls from one lifetime to another. As an organized faith, it developed around the same time as Buddhism, possibly between the ninth and sixth centuries B.C., although its adherents regard the faith as being eternal. Jain life is centered around the principle of non-violence, which is attained primarily through asceticism and detachment from physical reality.

Jains believe that every living being (not just humans) has an uncreated, eternal soul, which has the potential to develop into divinity (one who does so is called a *siddha*). Jainism also teaches the doctrine of *karma*, and every being is regarded as responsible for its own fate, based on its own actions. Like Buddhism and Yogin Hinduism, Jainism's goal is enlightenment and liberation (*moksh or nirvan*) from the cycle of rebirth through the shedding of all karma. When that happens, the soul is freed from earthly life and attains divine consciousness, which grants it infinite knowledge, power, vision, and bliss; thus it becomes a siddha. Karma is laid aside not by inaction or apathy, but by virtuous living, particularly non-violence. The path to liberation is through right faith (or vision), right knowledge, and right conduct, the "triple gems" of Jainism. It is also critical that followers learn to control their senses and minds, since these pull them away from the path of liberation.

Twenty-four souls who reached enlightenment are referred to as *tirthankar* (or *jina*), teachers who pass on the beliefs of Jainism (similar to the Hindi guru). The last such tirthankar was Mahavira, who is generally regarded as the one who set out the tenets of Jainism. *Tirthankar* literally means "ford-maker," because these people make it possible for human beings to ford across the "river of human misery," which comes from violence. Mahavira was the twenty-fourth in a line of the *tirthankara*, the first of whom was Rishabha. Together, these two are regarded as the founders of Jainism as it is now practiced.

The *tirthankara*, along with all teachers, Jain monastics (*sadhu*, a term also used in Hinduism and Buddhism), and enlightened beings who have passed on are highly revered by Jains, and it is believed that this veneration will help to grant knowledge of what they attained to believers. All of these divine people are venerated particularly in the recitation of the *namokar mantra*, a repetitive prayer in which the believer bows before these persons, though not by name.

Jains do not believe in any supreme being. In some sense all of nature is divine (pantheism), and of course individual souls may become divine (though only after becoming human first). Jainism is therefore in some sense a polytheistic system.

Jain monastics dedicate themselves to non-violence (*ahimsa*), truth (*satya*), non-stealing (*asteya*), chastity (*brahmachanga*), and non-possessiveness (*aparigraha*). In their worship at shrines and temples, Jains mainly bow before images of the tirthankara or other enlightened souls, and they may also recite mantras and other prayers, as well as anointing the images of the enlightened. There are two major sects of Jainism, the Shvetambaras ("white-clad") and Digambaras ("sky-clad," so-called because their monastics go naked).

Non-violence is the central virtue of Jain life, and some Jain monastics wear masks to prevent accidentally inhaling an insect or microbe. Some may not even eat vegetables (regarding them as having souls), but will only ingest fruit, nuts, and milk.

There is much in Jain belief and practice that is similar to Orthodox Christianity, such as the stress on not harming others, learning to control the mind and senses, giving up possessions in order to focus on what is most needful, and not indulging in pleasures. Likewise, the Orthodox believe that human beings may become divinized by proper living. Yet the Jain understanding of these things is incomplete because there is no personal God for whom these things are done. Likewise, divinization for Orthodoxy means union and communion with God, not ascendance through one's own virtues to a place of enlightenment.

Orthodoxy also rejects reincarnation, as noted earlier, and we do not believe that souls transmigrate from one being to another, especially not from humans to animals or plants. Human souls are unique and have only one lifetime on earth, which is given to them for repentance. There is only one God, the Holy Trinity.

Aside from the main Jain presence in India, there are also many Jains living in the West, including about 100,000 in the United States.

SIKHISM

Sikhism represents a kind of hybrid between Islam and Hinduism formed in sixteenth-century northern India, centered today in the Indian state of Punjab. Like Islam, Sikhism is strongly monotheistic. Like Islam, it also forbids the representation of God in images or bowing down before them. Another inheritance from Islam is an emphasis on the equality of all human beings. Sikhs reject the caste system of their neighboring Hindus.

Like Hindus, however, Sikhs believe in reincarnation and define ultimate salvation in terms common to some Hindus and most Buddhists—escape from the cycle of rebirth. Salvation is only possible through rigorous discipline and devotion to God, although not through separation from the world as in monasticism or the hermits of the Hindu Yogin tradition. Salvation is understood as being attained through an internal struggle in the heart—outward rituals, pilgrimages, and so forth are regarded as ultimately irrelevant. Salvation finally consists in absorption into God.

Sikh religious authority rests with a series of ten gurus who lived and taught during the sixteenth to eighteenth centuries. The "final guru" of Sikhism is the Guru Granth Sahib, also known as the *Adi Granth*, which is the Sikh scripture. Like Islam, Sikhism believes in the establishment of a theocratic state.

Orthodoxy shares with Sikhs the emphasis on the human heart as the locus of true spiritual work, but sees physical rituals as being part of the training of the heart. Further, salvation for the Orthodox is union and communion with God, not fusion with Him.

Sikhs are often recognizable by their long beards and hair. Their religion generally forbids cutting the hair, so the men bind it up in a turban to keep it out of the way, which makes them distinctively recognizable in the West. Many Sikh men and women have the same religious last name, *Singh* for men, meaning "tiger," and *Kaur* for women, meaning "princess." There are roughly 23 million Sikhs in the world, most of them living in Punjab in northern India. The word *Sikh* itself means "student."

SHINTO AND OTHER ANIMISM

Shinto is the traditional religion of Japan and was once its state religion. It is a type of animism and is therefore polytheistic. Animism itself is the belief that there are spirits in plants, animals, places, and even other humans that are worthy of worship. Some such spirits are considered purely local, while others are of a more universal character. Animists may believe in spirits that are connected with particular families, who could be the souls of dead ancestors. Although it is animist in its basic makeup, Shinto has been influenced by the philosophy of Confucianism and also by Buddhism. For many believers, following both Shinto and Buddhism is seen as perfectly acceptable, and two different altars, one dedicated to each faith, may be found in a home. This dual approach is quite common in Japan.

Shinto believers have a strong reverence for family and tradition. Family is the primary mechanism by which traditions are preserved, and many rituals are connected with key family events, such as birth, death, and marriage. Practitioners also have a strong reverence for the natural world, because of their belief in the spirits that inhabit it, which they call *kami*. To be close to nature is thus to be close to the *kami*. It is believed that every physical thing has its own *kami*, even mundane objects such as rocks. There are also *kami* for groups, such as a universal *kami* for all trees.

The religion places an emphasis on physical and ritual purity, which, if not observed, can disturb peace of mind and cause misfortune, possibly due to having offended a *kami*. This pursuit of cleanliness is not understood in an ethical sense, but rather in practical terms—if you want a peaceful and good life, you should be clean. Purification rituals are thus one of the major components of Shinto, and they may be performed for various reasons, such as placating an offended *kami* whose shrine had to be moved.

Those who follow both Shinto and Buddhism may believe in reincarnation and may interpret the *kami* as supernatural beings who are somehow caught in the cycle of rebirth.

Orthodox Christianity has a number of things in common with Shinto and other animistic faiths, most especially a reverence for nature. Like the Orthodox, Shinto priests will hold blessing rituals for homes, new businesses, groundbreakings, and so forth. Orthodox Christians, however, do not reverence nature because of a belief in spirits dwelling in various objects, but because we regard the whole creation as a gift from God, meant to be offered to Him in sacrifice. He then returns that creation to us as a means of salvation and sanctification, most especially in the Eucharist, but also in all other things that are offered to God for His blessing.

Orthodoxy also shares Shinto's high regard for family and tradition, though not for their own sake or for the sake of personal fulfillment. As with everything else, all is referenced back to the one true God, the Holy Trinity. Shinto practitioners, like the Orthodox, do not see themselves as isolated individuals, but rather as persons who are part of a whole, connected with an ancient tradition and having a duty to that tradition.

Shinto is also similar to Orthodoxy in its insistence that truth is not known primarily through the intellect, but rather through faith and experience.

There are ultimately many kinds of animism, which is a general term for polytheistic paganism with an emphasis on nature spirits. Shinto is one of the more developed varieties, whose practice enveloped a whole nation rather than only a single tribe, as is the case with many African animist religions.

MODERN WESTERN RELIGIONS

In the middle and at the end of the twentieth century, a fascination with Far Eastern religions and with faiths that had long since died grew in the West, particularly in the United States. This fascination is what Fr. Seraphim Rose refers to as "Vitalism" in one of his books (*Nihilism: The Root of the Revolution of the Modern Age*). Vitalism is essentially the pursuit of almost anything spiritual or philosophical that appears to have authenticity, most especially something hallowed by antiquity or by foreignness. It is a form of nihilism, because one of the key elements of the Vitalistic impulse is that there is no one, universal, absolute truth. Rather, there is only what is true "for me" or "for you."

Neo-Gnosticism

One of the forms of this Vitalist religious pursuit may be called neo-gnosticism. Like the ancient gnostics who distanced themselves from the Church, the new gnostics also see themselves as having a special, elite revelation the masses cannot hope to understand. Their actual beliefs vary widely, and perhaps the only thing most of them share is an aversion to Christianity, especially in its Western forms. Most so-called gnostics are isolated individuals who have discovered certain attractive teachings in a book or on the internet. Few actually exist as religious communities, though there are gnostic societies. Sociologically, gnosticism is especially attractive to academics and many who see themselves as intellectual elites.

These gnostics regard themselves as contemplatives and may draw upon numerous mystical practices and beliefs within multiple religious traditions that may otherwise contradict each other. Because of their religious elitism, critics and those who fail to understand these teachings may be looked upon by such gnostics as simply lesser beings who cannot hope to "get it."

Neo-gnosticism, like its ancient counterpart, is usually dualistic, seeing spiritual life as an attempt to be free of physical captivity. How this manifests itself may vary: Some gnostics may be sharply ascetical, like a Hindu Yogin, attempting to be free of the body. Others may instead embrace gross physical immorality, believing that what one does with the body is spiritually irrelevant.

Like the ancient gnostics, neo-gnostics stand in opposition to one of the basic truths of Orthodox Christianity, that the one God became man to save all of mankind. If gnostics do believe in Jesus, He is probably not God to them, but perhaps only a sort of intermediary connecting them to ultimate divine reality. The basic cure for neo-gnosticism is humility, because at its core, it is deeply arrogant in its basic religious premises.

Neo-Paganism and Wicca

Like neo-gnosticism, neo-paganism also varies considerably in terms of its beliefs and practices. The primary concept behind neo-paganism is that it is a revival of ancient religious life. It may be polytheistic, animistic, pantheistic, or otherwise. Most neo-pagans believe they are legitimately new followers of these ancient faiths, although in many cases we have scant evidence as to what such religions actually looked like or what their rituals were. Most neo-pagan faiths are actually reconstructions, reimagined creations based on what modern practitioners think the religions used to be like. Most followers are converts from Western Christian denominations. It is hard to count practitioners, but there may be as many as one to three million Wiccans and neo-pagans in the world, some of them united in denominational organizations.

Unlike their neo-gnostic counterparts, neo-pagans have a strong belief in the centrality of the physical world in their religious life. Many may worship nature itself or nature spirits. The basic goals of neo-paganism are like those of ancient paganism, namely, the pursuit of personal self-fulfillment and profit through religious acts.

The largest and most popular form of neo-paganism is Wicca, a term from Old English that referred to witchcraft. (*Wicca*, whose double-C is pronounced in Old English as soft "ch," is the origin of the modern English word *witch*.) Many Wiccans regard themselves as practicing an ancient religion, but its modern form is only a little over fifty years old and is based on the writings of nineteenth-century occultist Aleister Crowley. The primary activity of Wicca is in the study and casting of spells, and Wiccans may organize themselves into covens of witches and warlocks. Wiccans and other neo-pagans may sacrifice live animals as part of their practice.

Most Wiccans are ditheistic, believing in both a "God" and "Goddess," who are both closely identified with nature. Some may only believe in the "Goddess." Wicca and other forms of neo-paganism are often popular with young women, since the "mother goddess" image was a major part of ancient pagan religion. Thus, the particular brand of modern feminism that is shrill in its anti-masculinity helped to pave the way for the formation of these new religious movements.

Orthodox share with neo-pagans a love of nature, though for quite different reasons. Orthodoxy also offers neo-pagans something that was probably absent from their previous religious experience—a mystical tradition with a strongly physical side. Ultimately, though, the religion of neo-paganism must be understood as St. Paul put it in 1 Corinthians 10:20: "the things which the Gentiles sacrifice they sacrifice to demons and not to God, and I do not want you to have fellowship with demons." Neo-pagans and Wiccans are playing with forces they do not understand.

The basic Wiccan ethical affirmation is neutrality, expressed in this motto: "If it harm none, do as thou wilt." This is a sort of libertarian philosophy, which is attractive to many in the West. Do whatever you like, as long as you don't hurt anyone else. Of course, this is a highly individualistic understanding of human society. The Orthodox would contrast Wiccan morality with the far superior ethical urging of St. Augustine: "Love, and do what thou wilt."

Scientology

Scientology is a religion founded in California in 1954 by science fiction writer L. Ron Hubbard. As a religion, Scientology is mainly represented by the official Church of Scientology, although there are minor groups that have broken off. Whether Scientology is a religion or not is a matter of some debate. It describes itself as "applied religious philosophy," having little to say about God and mainly focusing on personal self-fulfillment. Scientology teaches that "Man is a spiritual being endowed with abilities well beyond those which he normally envisages. He is not only able to solve his own problems, accomplish his goals and gain lasting happiness, but also to achieve new states of awareness he may never have dreamed possible."

Scientology's basic teachings are outlined in Hubbard's book, *Dianetics: The Modern Science of Mental Health*, and are essentially a form of psychotherapy retooled in religious terms. Scientologists undergo a process known as "auditing" in which past experiences are recounted with another Scientologist in a one-on-one session. The person being "audited" is hooked up with electrodes to a machine called an "E-meter" which passes a low-level electrical current through the body. This process, Scientology says, helps to render a person "clear" of bad decisions and transgressions in life. Everything said by the person being "audited" is carefully recorded and stored in Scientology files.

As Scientologists progress deeper into the religion, they supposedly reach higher and higher states of spiritual "awareness" and gain abilities they didn't know they had. Each level requires larger and larger donations by members to the organization.

Scientology teaches that all evil that resides in a person is the result of the alien presence of "thetans," the souls of extra-terrestrial beings. These thetans came to Earth 75 million years ago when an extra-terrestrial galactic overlord named Xenu brought them here and stacked them around volcanoes. Xenu then set off a series of hydrogen bombs, making the volcanoes explode and sending the thetans careening all over the planet.

Perhaps one of the most telling quotes from Scientology founder L. Ron Hubbard was uttered in 1949: "I'd like to start a religion. That's where the money is." And in speaking of his career as a science fiction writer, he said, "Writing for a penny a word is ridiculous. If a man really wants to make a million dollars, the best way would be to start his own religion." Hubbard was not very successful as a science fiction writer, but he was able to put his inventiveness to more profitable use when he created Scientology, which besides its bizarre teachings about human nature and salvation, also teaches that humans evolved from clams. (A popular anti-Scientology website is named "Operation Clambake.")

For many reasons, but most especially because involvement with the organization is not free of charge, Scientology's status as a religion has been questioned, and in some countries it has been officially blacklisted by the government. Those who reveal its inner teachings to the public are often viciously pursued and persecuted by Scientology lawyers.

The differences from Orthodoxy should be fairly obvious, but one worth particularly pointing out is that the whole "religion," if it can truly be called that, is geared toward a totally self-centered manner of life. This approach, along with the secrecy and elitism of the higher levels of the organization, is probably what attracts so many celebrities to its ranks. In turn, the high profiles of celebrity Scientologists, such as Tom Cruise, help to attract others to the organization.

Scientology claims to have millions of members, but its actual membership probably numbers only in the tens of thousands.

CONCLUSIONS

Fr. John Garvey's book, *Seeds of the Word: Orthodox Thinking on Other Religions*, makes an important distinction between religious tolerance and religious compromise, as well as between firm religious belief and religious violence. These distinctions are often blurred in today's world, which is marked by relativistic ecumenism as well as religiously motivated terrorism. Nevertheless, the sober-minded Christian must keep both these distinctions in mind, firmly knowing and practicing the Christian faith while also genuinely loving others. Garvey also makes the point that St. Justin Martyr made in the second century, namely, that while we believe that Orthodox Christianity is the fullness of God's revelation to mankind, Orthodox Christians nevertheless also believe that God is working in all people throughout all of history. That work will manifest itself in a number of ways, including within other religions.

That being said, I believe that each of us has much to learn from other religious traditions. I say this as an individual person writing to other individuals. The Church, which includes Christ as Head and chief member, does not have any learning to do, because God has revealed Himself within His Church, leading the Apostles into all truth (John 16:13). There is nothing else that needs to be "taught" to the Church other than what it received from Christ.

Yet each of us as Christians working out our salvation in fear and trembling (Phil. 2:12) can come to knowledge of Christ by many means. The clearest and most direct way is within the Church, but a Christian functioning within the Church may be exposed to the Church's truth even outside the visible boundaries of the Church. This is why each of us needs to remain open to transformation and personal change, because none of us here on earth has yet attained the fullness of our salvation (Phil. 3:12). But because all truth is God's truth—after all, Truth is Christ (John 14:6)—whatever truth we encounter is ultimately not a contradiction to the Orthodox faith but rather an expression of it. If it seems to contradict the faith, then we have misunderstood either what we have encountered or the faith itself; or else we have mistaken falsehood for truth.

All of this must add up to humility for each of us, especially when we encounter people who believe in other faiths. Some religious groups, such as the Church of Scientology, may strike us as deeply ridiculous, but in relating to such people, we need to keep in mind that all people are created according to Christ, the image of the invisible God (Gen. 1:27; Col. 1:15). As such, all of them are meant for communion with Him, and all are deserving of our love, honor, and respect. The best approach to bringing the fullness of the Gospel to people of other faiths is to affirm what we have in common and to expand on that common truth to reveal the wholeness of Orthodoxy. Even Scientology shares a basic belief in the brokenness of mankind and his need for healing.

May God grant us humility, patience, and love as we seek to deepen our own experience of salvation and to bring that experience to others.

Epilogue

In the course of this book, we have examined the teachings and practices of well over a hundred religions, denominations, sects, and heretical groups, sometimes in brief and sometimes with more detail. Truly, though, we have only scratched the surface of most of them. If we had believers from these traditions reading along with us, we would most likely be accused of oversimplifying, generalizing, and misinterpreting who they are.

Though I have tried my best to represent them as fairly as I can with the resources at my disposal, misrepresentation is always unavoidable to a certain extent. There are two reasons for this. First, it is because detailed understanding of a religion can take a whole lifetime; it is impossible to say that you truly know a religion unless you have lived it and lived it well. Second, it is also because in this work we have explicitly taken it upon ourselves to look at these religions with the eyes of Orthodox Christianity, not from some theoretical, impartial viewpoint, free of all bias. I believe such impartiality is ultimately impossible, anyway.

What we can say with some certainty, however, is that each of these religions constitutes a coherent theological and spiritual world for its believers. We can speculate on the inner spiritual state of believers with whom we disagree, but for most serious Muslims, Mormons, Methodists, Mennonites, and Mandaeans, it is self-evident that what they believe is correct. Even if they have never taken the time to examine their beliefs critically, sincere followers of any religion continue to follow it because they believe it is true.

For any religious believer, such belief is never entirely founded on concrete evidence. Even if it were, the philosopher of epistemology might ask such people how they absolutely know they can trust their senses. How do you know what you see and hear is what's really there? Therefore, all religious belief—in fact, all belief, whether religious or not—is founded upon faith. Faith is a trust built on a mysterious and hard-to-analyze mixture of evidence, interpretation, experience, relationship, and reason. So while we may criticize other religions and their theology, we still must look upon their followers as God's children, assuming they are acting in good faith on what they believe to be true.

In speaking about these many dozens of religious groups, we have employed reason, history, and the Scripture to criticize their teachings and practices. It is evident to me, of course, that Orthodox Christianity is right and all the rest of these groups are at least partly wrong (some more than others). But it is also possible that someone else may be exposed to the same set of evidence and draw entirely different conclusions. There are much smarter, more learned, and more sincere people than I who have done so. But since we know that very smart, learned, and sincere people often disagree with one another, we cannot conclude that choosing the wrong religion is only a matter of intelligence, ignorance, or personal moral failing. There are people of goodwill in all these groups. There are quite educated people in all these groups. There are many sincere people in all these groups.

While I want every person in the world to become an Orthodox Christian, I have no illusions that the words written in this book will magically make people want to convert to Orthodox Christianity. Words in any book, even one as powerful as the Bible, can only ever help to map out the path or to clear away some of the obstacles. This latter goal, the clearing of obstacles, is really the point of this book. The path must still be walked, and how one finds the way to it and how one walks it is always a precious secret really known only to God. To try to unpack it in its entirety and display it for the whole world would be to do violence to its integrity—and is impossible, anyway.

What I think we have to see is that there is a mysterious border country between these different religions. In that strange country is the locus of conversion. In that mysterious place, reason, history, Scripture, experience, expectation, desire, and relationship may all steer the traveler in one direction or another. But what we cannot track and cannot chart is the working of the Holy Spirit, who, we believe, is at work in every human being.

Our task, therefore, as children of God who love our brothers and sisters and wish them to know the love and salvation of God, is to do what we can to nudge folks into that border country. But what we must also realize is that the critical part is played by both God and the person himself. The only authenticator of the Gospel is the One to whom it points. And once it is authenticated within the human person, it is up to him either to act on it or not. Conversion is always an act of the human will and also always a miracle. The truth of the Gospel is made apparent through divine intervention.

Our job is to preach the Gospel.

Appendix I

Atheism and Agnosticism

Perhaps the most frequent request I received in the course of doing the *Orthodoxy and Heterodoxy* podcast series was to address atheism and agnosticism. But I hadn't prepared any material on those viewpoints, because they're not religions. Yes, I agree with those who say that being an atheist or agnostic requires a certain kind of faith, but that doesn't really make them religions. Nevertheless, because it is likely that we will encounter people in our lives who describe themselves as atheists and agnostics, it seemed a good idea to add something to this material in its written form.

First, we have to realize that these terms—*atheist* and *agnostic*—are used by people to mean a number of different (but related) things. Here are some examples:

- "I do not believe that there is a god."
- "I believe that there is no god."
- "I have no beliefs that have anything to do with a god."
- "I know that there is no god."
- "I have seen no evidence that there is a god."
- "I don't know whether there is a god."
- "I cannot know whether there is a god."
- "No one can know whether there is a god."
- "If there is a god, I don't like him and want nothing to do with him."
- "I don't believe in *your* god."
- "People in that church are hypocrites and I want nothing to do with them."
- "Religious people have done bad things in the name of their god."

There are a lot of assumptions (many of them simply factually wrong or incomplete) that lie behind many of those statements. For instance, a lot of atheists have rejected faith in God because they don't like the way God has been presented to them—usually as a tyrannical, arbitrary punisher. The best response to that problem is simply to show them that Orthodoxy does not believe in that "God," either. God loves everyone and wants to heal everyone, and that healing is available to all who will cooperate with Him.

Another of the most common objections is that religious people do bad things, sometimes in the name of their religion. I recall seeing, "GOD SAVE ME FROM YOUR FOLLOWERS," scrawled on the inside of a bathroom stall once while traveling. This objection has some genuine substance to it, but there is a logical fallacy here. The fact that a person who says he's a believer does something bad doesn't mean that there is no God or that his religion is false. While there are some religions that demand bad things (such as human sacrifice), the bad person under discussion may actually be violating his own religion. (A good example here is that of clergy who abuse children. I have never heard of one whose religion condoned that behavior.) At the same time, anyone who objects to religion because of killing in religious wars has only to consider the twentieth century's bloodbath at the hands of atheistic governments. If Stalin doesn't delegitimize all atheism, neither should the Inquisition delegitimize all religion. Sometimes, we do have to ask God to save us from His followers, because those people are not actually following Him.

Probably the biggest issue with atheists and agnostics is the question of evidence. Where exactly is this God that believers claim to know? That is, indeed, the crux of the matter. Reason should make it apparent that no one can honestly say, "I know that there is no god." Why? Saying such a thing would require that someone have knowledge of absolutely everything there is. A needle may be placed in a haystack, but unless absolutely every piece of hay is examined separately, you cannot say, "There is no needle there."

While a person dedicated to finding that needle does have the possibility of being that thorough, no human being could ever examine the whole universe to see if there is a god anywhere in it. Not only would that require the ability simultaneously to observe all the parts of reality that we can theorize as existing, but it would also require that we have perfect knowledge of everything that might exist at all in any shape. What if there are other dimensions of reality that are not bounded by our universe? And even if we knew all the possible space that needed to be explored, do we have the right kinds of tools to detect what is present in it? Or what if we detected a god but didn't know that was whom we were seeing?

The issue here is what tools are being used to see the evidence. The Bible itself tells us that some things can only be seen with eyes of faith. Orthodoxy also teaches that some knowledge only comes through experience, usually only through a long struggle in asceticism and repentance. The Lord Jesus says it is the "pure in heart" who see God (Matt. 5:8).

So how do we help people to see God who just don't see Him? It's tough to insist that they have to enter the Church and embark on a lifelong journey of asceticism before they'll really see God. Few people will take you up on that invitation. Nevertheless, I believe that the key is in the words of Christ, that seeing God requires purity of heart. Most atheists and agnostics will at least acknowledge that morality is a good thing, even if they refuse to adhere to it because of the authority of the Christian tradition. Such a person can be encouraged toward selflessness, which purifies the heart when it is undertaken, even if only partially, opening it up to be touched by the divine light.

At the same time, the most powerful evangelistic strategy with atheists and agnostics is simply to love them and pray earnestly for them. They probably are tired of having people try to convert them, so it's unlikely that any arguments will win them over. They are also probably burned out by the hypocrisy of so-called believers. But there is no defense against love. Words can always contend with words, but no word can contend with life.

A life that is lived in authentic love will preach the Gospel to all those around. If someone doesn't want to believe, talking to him will never make him believe. But giving yourself selflessly for him may well provoke some questions within that he's never considered before. Being kind to him when you are not required to do so may inspire him to want to know the Source of your kindness. Giving him freedom when every other religious person has tried to trap him may make an impact he's never felt before.

I think one of the mistakes many of us make (including myself) when speaking with atheists, agnostics, or any person who does not share our faith is to believe that we can argue them into seeing the truth. I do not believe this is possible. I have never known anyone who was successfully argued into a lasting faith.

There actually were two people I argued to the point that they were received into the Orthodox Church. With the force of reason, history, and other evidence, I convinced them mentally that Orthodoxy was the one, true Church of Jesus Christ. But now neither is in the Church. They left. To be sure, their choices are their own responsibility, but I take their departure as a warning to myself, all the same.

Christian faith is built on an encounter with the God-man Jesus Christ. It is not built on stacking up enough incontrovertible evidence interpreted correctly through reason that anyone who comes upon such a stack will have no choice but to become Christian. Because faith is built on an encounter, it is not something that can ever be coerced, whether by force of reason or any other kind of force.

To be converted to Jesus Christ means that a human person encounters Him and is mysteriously drawn to trust Him and to unite with Him. All we can do is to open the path between that person and Christ, remembering that both persons have the freedom not to make the encounter. Our strongest evangelistic tools are love and prayer.

Appendix II

Orthodoxy Quick Reference

1. **The Holy Trinity**
   - One God.
   - God is uncreated, existing before all created things.
   - God is three Persons, one in Essence.
   - All three Persons are absolutely equal.
   - All attributes of God are either unique to each Person (e.g., Fatherhood) or common to all three (e.g., perfection).
   - The Father is the eternal Source of the Godhead. The Son is begotten of the Father, while the Spirit proceeds from the Father.
   - God is unknowable essence and knowable energies.

2. **Jesus Christ**
   - Jesus Christ is the Son of God, the Second Person of the Trinity.
   - He is fully divine and of one essence with the Father.
   - He is fully human and of one essence with mankind.
   - He is one Person in two natures.
   - He truly was born, lived, died, and bodily rose from the dead.
   - He is the Messiah prophesied in the Hebrew Scriptures.

3. **The Church**
   - There is only one Church, the Orthodox Church.
   - The Church is the Body of Christ. He is a member and its only Head.
   - Salvation is in and through the Church.
   - Salvation is *theosis* ("deification," "divinization"), becoming more like God in union with Him.
   - Salvation is a change not merely in status, but in actual being.
   - Salvation is by God's power but only with man's active cooperation, termed *synergy*.

- The sacraments really communicate grace by means of their administration from the episcopacy, who are successors to the Apostles.
- Christ will return again, and that will be the end of time. At that time, all the dead will rise, the righteous to a resurrection of life and the wicked to a resurrection of death.

Appendix III

Heresy Quick Reference

1. **Docetism**—Jesus was God, but only "appeared" to be human.
2. **Judaizing**—Christians should become Jews first or follow more of the Jewish Law.
3. **Gnosticism**—"Knowledge" saves and may be available only to a select few. Highly dualistic.
4. **Marcionism**—Rejection of Hebrew "god" in favor of New Testament "god."
5. **Montanism**—Ecstatic spiritual experiences sought out, new revelation through "prophet" Montanus.
6. **Manichaeism**—Persian gnostic religion, highly dualistic.
7. **Sabellianism**—Father, Son, and Holy Spirit are only "modes" or "masks" of one divine Person.
8. **Novatianism**—People who apostatize or commit serious sin can never be absolved.
9. **Donatism**—Personal moral unworthiness invalidates the sacraments of clergy (even if repentant).
10. **Arianism**—Christ is not God, but only the highest created being.
11. **Chiliasm**—Christ will reign for a literal one thousand years after the Second Coming.
12. **Apollinarianism**—Christ did not have a human soul, but the Logos fulfilled that role.
13. **Pneumatomachianism**—The Holy Spirit is not divine, but a creature.
14. **Pelagianism**—Man can save himself without divine grace.
15. **Nestorianism**—Jesus Christ is two persons "conjoined."
16. **Monophysitism**—Jesus Christ has one, hybrid nature, half God and half man.
17. **Apokatastasis**—All will be saved, even if they reject God.
18. **Origenism**—A set of Platonized cosmological teachings and speculations.
19. **Monothelitism**—Jesus had only one will, the divine.

20. **Monoenergism**—Jesus had only one energy, the divine.
21. **Iconoclasm**—Icons should be removed from churches and destroyed.
22. **Filioquism**—The Holy Spirit proceeds eternally from the Father *and the Son*.
23. **Barlaamism**—Rejection of hesychasm, assertion that highest knowledge is mental/philosophical.
24. **Ethnophyletism**—Church governance should be based on ethnic rather than geographic divisions.

Appendix IV

Further Reading on Roman Catholicism

A. ORTHODOX SOURCES

Books

Carlton, Clark. *The Truth: What Every Roman Catholic Should Know About the Orthodox Church.* Salisbury, MA: Regina Orthodox Press, 1999.

Clement, Olivier. *You Are Peter: An Orthodox Reflection on the Exercise of Papal Primacy.* New City Press, 2003.

Guettée, Abbé. *The Papacy: Its Historic Origin and Primitive Relations.*

Meyendorff, John, ed. *The Primacy of Peter: Essays in Ecclesiology and the Early Church.* Crestwood, NY: St. Vladimir's Seminary Press, 1992.

Papadakis, Aristeides. *The Christian East and the Rise of the Papacy: The Church 1071–1453 A.D.* Crestwood, NY: St. Vladimir's Seminary Press, 1994.

Pelikan, Jaroslav. *The Christian Tradition: A History of the Development of Doctrine, Vol. 3: The Growth of Medieval Theology (600–1300).* University of Chicago Press, 1980.

Romanides, John. *The Ancestral Sin.* Zephyr Publishing, 2002.

Runciman, Steven. *The Eastern Schism: A Study of the Papacy and the Eastern Churches During the XIth and XIIth Centuries.* Wipf & Stock Publishers, 2005.

Sherrard, Philip. *Church, Papacy and Schism: A Theological Enquiry.* Limni, Evia, Greece: Denise Harvey, 1996.

Sherrard, Philip. *The Greek East and Latin West: A Study in the Christian Tradition.* Limni, Evia, Greece: Denise Harvey, 1995.

Whelton, Michael. *Popes and Patriarchs: An Orthodox Perspective on Roman Catholic Claims*. Ben Lomond, CA: Conciliar Press, 2006.

Whelton, Michael. *Two Paths: Papal Monarchy—Collegial Tradition: Rome's Claim of Papal Supremacy in the Light of Orthodox Teaching*. Salisbury, MA: Regina Orthodox Press, 2001.

Yannaras, Christos. *The Freedom of Morality*. Crestwood, NY: St. Vladimir's Seminary Press, 1984.

Young, Fr. Alexey. [Various titles, incl. *The Rush to Embrace, The Great Divide* and *Christianity or Papism?*]

Websites

For Roman Catholic Inquirers: http://www.orthodoxinfo.com/inquirers/inq_rc.aspx

The *Filioque*: http://www.geocities.com/trvalentine/orthodox/filioquemain.html

What are the Differences...?: http://www.ocf.org/OrthodoxPage/reading/ortho_cath.html

The Great Schism: http://www.fatheralexander.org/booklets/english/history_timothy_ware_1.htm#n4

B. ROMAN CATHOLIC SOURCES

Vatican Website: http://www.vatican.va/

Vatican Resource Library: http://www.vatican.va/archive/index.htm

Catechism of the Catholic Church: http://www.vatican.va/archive/ccc_css/archive/catechism/ccc_toc.htm

James Likoudis (polemicist convert from Orthodoxy): http://credo.stormloader.com/jlindex.htm (Likoudis also has a number of anti-Orthodox books)

Dave Armstrong (RC apologist): http://socrates58.blogspot.com/2006/11/orthodoxy-eastern-index-page.html

C. ONLINE REFERENCES

Internet Medieval Sourcebook: http://www.fordham.edu/halsall/sbook.html
OrthodoxWiki: http://www.orthodoxwiki.org/

The list above is by no means exhaustive. The reader is admonished to dig deep and focus on primary sources when exploring this subject.

Appendix V

Timeline of Major Dates for Orthodox/ Roman Catholic Relations

ca. AD 37–53 Episcopacy of St. Peter in Antioch.

50 Apostolic Council of Jerusalem overrules St. Peter's Judaizing.

64 Martyrdom of St. Peter in Rome.

67 Election of St. Linus, first bishop of Rome.

135 First recorded use of title *pope* by a Roman bishop (Hyginus).

255 St. Cyprian of Carthage rejects Pope Stephen I's ruling on baptism by heretics.

325 Original Nicene Creed ratified at First Ecumenical Council.

330 Founding of Constantinople as New Rome, renaming the city of Byzantium.

357 Pope Liberius signs semi-Arian creed (possibly under duress).

379 Emperor Gratian permits Roman pope authority over neighboring bishops.

381 Nicene Creed expanded at Second Ecumenical Council.

382 First use of papal title *Pontifex Maximus* (formerly a pagan religious title reserved to the emperor).

410 Rome sacked by Visigoth invaders.

417 Pope Zosimus waffles on Pelagianism.

451 Fourth Ecumenical Council notes that Rome is given primacy because it is "the imperial city"; *Tome* of Pope St. Leo I endorsed by Council after review.

455 Rome sacked by Vandals.

589 Insertion of *Filioque* into Nicene Creed by local council in Toledo, Spain.

ca. 590–604   Pope St. Gregory the Great rejects the title of "universal bishop" for any bishop.

680–681   Sixth Ecumenical Council anathematizes Pope Honorius as a Monothelite heretic.

710   Last papal visit to Constantinople until 1967.

ca. 750   Forging of the *Donation of Constantine*, a false document claiming to be from St. Constantine granting universal secular power to the pope and his successors.

752   Founding of Papal States (lasting until 1870).

792   Charles the Great ("Charlemagne") accuses "Greeks" (who called themselves "Romans") of deleting *Filioque* from original Creed.

800   Usurpation of Western Roman Empire by Charles the Great.

809   Pope Leo III forbids addition of *Filioque* to Creed and has original Creed in both Greek and Latin inscribed on silver tablets displayed in Rome.

869–870   Council in Constantinople (endorsed by papacy) deposes St. Photius the Great.

879–880   Council in Constantinople (endorsed by papacy) reinstates St. Photius and anathematizes any changes to Nicene Creed, including the *Filioque*.

962   Founding of Holy Roman Empire.

1014   First use of *Filioque* by Pope of Rome, at coronation of Holy Roman Emperor Henry II.

1054   Excommunication of Ecumenical Patriarch Michael Cerularius by Cardinal Humbert, papal legate—the conventional date point of the Great Schism. Michael returns the favor by excommunicating the pope (who had died, rendering his legate's authority null).

1066   Invasion of England by Duke William of Normandy, carrying papal banner and with papal blessing as a crusade against the "erring" English church, engineered by Hildebrand, archdeacon of Rome.

1073–85   Hildebrand becomes Pope Gregory VII and expands Gregorian Reforms (which had begun earlier but were named for him), the largest increase of papal power in history, including the claim to be able to depose secular rulers.

1075   Pope Gregory VII issues *Dictatus papae,* an extreme statement of papal power.

1095–1522   Crusades promise salvation to warriors from the West.

1149   Beginning of the use of the term *transubstantiation.*

1180   Last formal reception of Latins to communion at an Orthodox altar, in Antioch.

1182   Marionites in Lebanon (formerly Monothelite heretics) submit to Rome.

1204   Fourth Crusade sacks Constantinople; Crusaders set up Latin Empire and Latin Patriarchate of Constantinople (lasting until 1261).

1274   Council of Lyons fails to force Orthodox submission to papacy.

1287   Last record of Benedictine monastery on Mount Athos.

1302   Papal bull *Unam Sanctam* declares submission to pope necessary for salvation.

1341–51   Councils in Constantinople vindicate Palamite theology of hesychasm against Barlaamist philosophy.

1378   Beginning of Western "Great Schism," during which there are eventually three rival popes.

1414–18   Council of Constance ends Western "Great Schism."

1439   Council of Florence fails to force Orthodox submission to papacy and confesses purgatory as dogma.

1444   Catholic priest Lorenzo Valla proves *Donation of Constantine* a forgery.

1453   Fall of Constantinople to Ottoman Turks; numerous Greek scholars flee to West, triggering European Renaissance.

1545–63   Council of Trent answers charges of Protestant Reformation.

1582   Institution of Gregorian calendar.

1596   Union of Brest-Litovsk, creation of the Unia (Eastern/ Byzantine/Greek Catholics).

1724   Melkite Schism, in which many Antiochian Orthodox become Greek Catholics.

1854   Declaration of immaculate conception of Mary as dogma.

1870   Declaration of papal infallibility as dogma at First Vatican Council.

1946   State-sponsored synod held in Ukraine dissolves the Union of Brest-Litovsk and integrates the Ukrainian Greek Catholic Church into the Russian Orthodox Church, with Soviet authorities arresting resisters or deporting them to Siberia.

1950   Declaration of bodily assumption of Mary as dogma.

1962–65   Vatican II institutes major reforms, especially liturgical, in Roman Catholic Church.

1964   Mutual lifting of excommunications by Patriarch Athenagoras I and Pope Paul VI.

1979   Joint Commission of Orthodox and Roman Catholic Churches for Theological Dialogue established.

1995   Pope John Paul II issues *Orientale Lumen*, encouraging East-West union.

2001   Pope John Paul II apologizes to Orthodox for Fourth Crusade.

2004   Relics of Ss. John Chrysostom and Gregory the Theologian returned to Constantinople from Rome (after having been stolen by Crusaders).

2006   Pope Benedict XVI drops title *Patriarch of the West*.

Appendix VI

Further Reading on Protestantism

A. ORTHODOX SOURCES

Bajis, Jordan. *Common Ground: An Introduction to Eastern Christianity for the American Christian*. Light & Life Publishing, 1991.

Bernstein, Fr. A. James. *Which Came First, the Church or the New Testament?* Conciliar Press Topical Series Booklet.

Carlton, Clark. *The Way: What Every Protestant Should Know About the Orthodox Church*. Salisbury, MA: Regina Orthodox Press, 1997.

Gallatin, Matthew. *Thirsting for God in a Land of Shallow Wells*. Conciliar Press, 2002.

Gillquist, Peter. *Becoming Orthodox: A Journey to the Ancient Christian Faith*. Conciliar Press, 1992.

Gillquist, Peter, ed. *Coming Home: Why Protestant Clergy Are Becoming Orthodox*. Conciliar Press, 1995.

Mastrontonis, George, trans. *Augsburg and Constantinople: The Correspondence between the Tubingen Theologians and Patriarch Jeremiah II of Constantinople on the Augsburg Confession*. Holy Cross Orthodox Press, 2005.

Pelikan, Jaroslav. *The Christian Tradition: A History of the Development of Doctrine, Vol. 4: Reformation of Church and Dogma (1300–1700)*. University of Chicago Press, 1985.

Rose, Fr. Seraphim. *Orthodoxy and the Religion of the Future*. St. Herman of Alaska Brotherhood, 1996.

Rose, Fr. Seraphim. *The Place of Blessed Augustine in the Orthodox Church*. Platina, CA: St. Herman of Alaska Brotherhood, 1996.

Schaeffer, Frank. *Dancing Alone: The Quest for Orthodox Faith in the Age of False Religion*. Regina Orthodox Press, 2002.

Schmemann, Alexander. *For the Life of the World: Sacraments and Orthodoxy*. St. Vladimir's Seminary Press, 1997.

B. PROTESTANT SOURCES

Carroll, J. M. *The Trail of Blood*, 1931. Online at: http://bryanstation.com/trail_of_blood.htm

Clendenin, Daniel. *Eastern Orthodoxy: A Western Perspective*. Baker Academic, 2003.

Clendenin, Daniel. *Why I'm Not Orthodox*. Online at: http://uecb.by.ru/eng/archive/orthodox1.htm

Lee, Philip J. *Against the Protestant Gnostics*. New York: Oxford University Press, 1987.

Letham, Robert. *Through Western Eyes—Eastern Orthodoxy: A Reformed Perspective*. Mentor, 2007.

Spann, Matt. *Witnessing to People of Eastern Orthodox Background: Turning Barriers of Belief into Bridges to Personal Faith*, 2001. Online at: http://www.namb.net/evangelism/iev/PDF/BB_E_Orthodox_Manual.pdf

Tradition Betrayed: Eastern Orthodoxy Examined in the Light of the Apostolic Faith (*Credenda/Agenda* Vol. 6, No. 5): http://www.credenda.org/old/issues/cont6-5.htm see also response at http://www.orthodoxinfo.com/inquirers/credenda_response.aspx

C. WEBSITES

http://www.orthodoxinfo.com/inquirers/

Life of St. Elizabeth the New Martyr: http://www.orthodoxwiki.org/Elizabeth_the_New_Martyr

Tibbs, Eve. *16th Century Lutheran & Orthodox Dialogue*. http://www.stpaulsirvine.org/html/lutheran.htm

http://www.orthodoxwiki.org/

Wikipedia: http://en.wikipedia.org/wiki/History_of_Protestantism
http://en.wikipedia.org/wiki/Radical_Reformation
http://en.wikipedia.org/wiki/Christian_revival
http://en.wikipedia.org/wiki/Evangelicalism
http://en.wikipedia.org/wiki/Pentecostalism

The Oxford Dictionary of the Christian Church is also an excellent and thorough resource on numerous movements and figures.

The list above is by no means exhaustive. The reader is admonished to dig deep and focus on primary sources when exploring this subject.

Appendix VII

Further Reading on Non-Mainstream Christians

A. ORTHODOX SOURCES

Books

Pelikan, Jaroslav. *The Christian Tradition: A History of the Development of Doctrine, Vol. 5: Christian Doctrine and Modern Culture (Since 1700)*. University of Chicago Press, 1989. (written while Pelikan was still Lutheran)

Morris, John W. *Cultist at My Door*. Conciliar Press Topical Series Booklet.

Websites

OrthodoxWiki: Mormonism: http://orthodoxwiki.org/Mormonism

OrthodoxWiki: Jehovah's Witnesses: http://orthodoxwiki.org/Jehovah's_Witnesses

B. OTHER SOURCES

Christadelphia World Wide: http://www.christadelphia.org/

Jehovah's Witnesses: http://www.watchtower.org/

Mother Church of Christian Science: http://www.tfccs.com/

Mormonism:

   Official site: http://www.mormon.org/

   Criticism: http://en.wikipedia.org/wiki/Criticism_of_the_Latter_Day_Saint_movement

Utah Lighthouse Ministry: http://www.utlm.org/ (Detailed, extensive LDS criticism from a descendant of Brigham Young and her husband)
ReligionFacts: http://www.religionfacts.com/
Swedenborgian Church: http://www.swedenborg.org/
Unification Church: http://www.unification.org/
Unitarian Universalist Association: http://www.uua.org/

The list above is by no means exhaustive. The reader is admonished to dig deep and focus on primary sources when exploring this subject. There is also some relevant material in the *Oxford Dictionary of the Christian Church*.

There are not many Orthodox sources on these non-mainstream Christian groups.

Appendix VIII

Further Reading on Non-Christian Religions

A. ORTHODOX SOURCES

Books

Bernstein, Fr. A. James. *Surprised by Christ: My Journey from Judaism to Orthodox Christianity*. Ben Lomond, CA: Conciliar Press, 2008.

Christensen, Hmk. Damascene. *Christ the Eternal Tao*. St. Herman of Alaska Brotherhood, 2004.

Farasiotis, Dionysios. *The Gurus, the Young Man, and Elder Paisios*. St. Herman of Alaska Brotherhood, 2008.

Garvey, John. *Seeds of the Word: Orthodox Thinking on Other Religions*. Crestwood, NY: St. Vladimir's Seminary Press, 2005.

Metwalli, Nahed Mahmoud. *Islam Encounters Christ*. Minneapolis, MN: Light & Life Publishing, 2002.

Pelikan, Jaroslav. *The Christian Tradition: A History of the Development of Doctrine, Vol. 1: The Emergence of the Catholic Tradition (100–600)*. University of Chicago Press, 1975, pp. 11–27, "The True Israel."

Rose, Eugene. *Nihilism: The Root of the Revolution of the Modern Age*. St. Herman of Alaska Brotherhood, 1994. Online at: http://www.columbia.edu/cu/augustine/arch/nihilism.html

Rose, Fr. Seraphim. *Orthodoxy and the Religion of the Future*. St. Herman of Alaska Brotherhood, 1996.

Vaporis, Nomikos Michael. *Witnesses for Christ: Orthodox Christian Neomartyrs of the Ottoman Period (1437–1860)*. Crestwood, NY: St. Vladimir's Seminary Press, 2000.

Websites

Buddhism and Eastern asceticism compared to Orthodox asceticism: http://www.pravoslavie.ru/english/7423.htm

Orthodox Christian View of Non-Christian Religions: http://www.goarch.org/ourfaith/ourfaith8089

Orthodoxy and the Religion of the Future (excerpts): http://www.orthodox-photos.com/readings/future/ (Includes sections on Hinduism, Buddhism, etc.)

Surprised by Christ (Judaism to Orthodox Christianity): http://www.surprisedbychrist.com/

B. OTHER SOURCES

Hodgson, Marshall G. S. *The Venture of Islam (3 vols.)*. University of Chicago Press, 1974.

Operation Clambake: The Inner Secrets of Scientology: http://www.xenu.net/

Ye'or, Bat. *The Decline of Eastern Christianity Under Islam: From Jihad to Dhimmitude: Seventh–Twentieth Century*. Fairleigh Dickinson University Press, 1996.

C. OTHER REFERENCES

Religion Facts: http://www.religionfacts.com/
    Big Religion Chart: http://www.religionfacts.com/big_religion_chart.htm

The list above is by no means exhaustive. The reader is admonished to dig deep and focus on primary sources when exploring this subject.

(Page numbers refer to beginning of section in which this subject is discussed, not the exact page number)

Photo by Jane Larsen

About the Author

The Rev. Fr. Andrew Stephen Damick is pastor of St. Paul Orthodox Church in Emmaus, Pennsylvania. He also lectures widely on Orthodox evangelism, history, ecology, comparative theology, and localism. He is a founding member and one of the associate directors of the Society for Orthodox Christian History in the Americas. Fr. Andrew hosts the *Orthodoxy and Heterodoxy* and *Roads from Emmaus* podcast series, as well as writing the *Roads from Emmaus* weblog. He lives in Emmaus with his wife Kh. Nicole and their children.